Wooden Spoon
Yearbook 2020

RUGBY WORLD CUP
SPECIAL

Wooden Spoon

RUGBY WORLD Yearbook 2020

RUGBY WORLD CUP SPECIAL

EDITOR
Ian Robertson

PHOTOGRAPHS
Getty Images
and Fotosport

Published in the UK in 2019 by
Lennard Publishing, an imprint of
Lennard Associates Ltd,
Mackerye End,
Harpenden, Herts AL5 5DR

email: orders@lennardqap.co.uk

Distributed by G2 Entertainment
c/o Orca Book Services
160 Eastern Avenue, Milton Park
Abingdon, OX14 4SB

ISBN: 978-1-78281-625-6

Production editor: Donald Sommerville
Text and cover design: Paul Cooper

The publishers would like to thank the photograhers of Getty Images for providing many of the
photographs for this book: Anthony An-Yeung, Odd Andersen/AFP, The Ashari Shimbun, Athena Pictures,
Sam Barnes/Sportsfile, Sean Botterill, Gabriel Bouys/AFP, Henry Browne, Matt Browne/Sportsfile, Geoff
Caddick/AFP, Lynne Cameron, Jean Catuffe, Ian Cook/Camerasport, Charlie Crowhurst, Adrian
Dennis/AFP, Marcello Endelli/World Rugby, Javier Escobar/NurPhoto, Franck Fife/AFP, Stu Forster,
Laurence Griffiths, Richard Heathcote/World Rugby, Mike Hewitt, Ken Ishii, Mark Kolbe, Matthew Lewis,
Warren Little/World Rugby, Tony Marshall, Charles McQuillan, Behrouz Mehri/AFP, Buda Mendes/World
Rugby, Filippo Monteforte, Brendan Moran/Sportsfile, Pablo Morano/MB Media, Dan Mullan, Koki
Nagahama, Francois Nel/World Rugby, Kazuhiro Nogi/AFP, Amilcar Orfali, Hannah Peters, Anne-
Christine Poujoulat/AFP, Alberto Pozzoli/AFP, Adam Pretty, David Ramos/World Rugby, David Rogers,
Clive Rose/World Rugby, Will Russell, Christophe Simon/AFP, Cameron Spencer, Michel Steele, Charly
Triballeau/AFP, Rodrigo Valle, Levan Verdzeuli, Wallis/Icon Sport, Lee Warren /Gallo Images, William
West/AFP, Dave Winter/Icon Sport. Thanks also to Fotosport photographers David Gibson, Hiro Irie, Alain
Mounic and Steve Haag Sports/Holluywoodbets. The publishers are grateful to Chris Thau and David
Stewart for providing additional illustrative material.

A special thank you to Terry Cooper for assembling the quotes from the quarter-finals, semi-finals and
final of RWC 2019.

Printed and bound in Italy
by L.E.G.O. S.p.A

CONTENTS

The Saracens Sport Foundation aims to inspire communities and change lives through the power of sport. We are dedicated to bringing about positive change, engaging with and challenging participants of all ages to lead active, healthy and rewarding lives.

Our programmes address specific social needs within the North London and Hertforshire community by encouraging increased participation in sport and physical activity; breaking down barriers to participation for specific excluded groups, developing interventions to address health issues and developing pathways into education and employment.

Sport has the ability to make a difference in people's lives that goes well beyond the sporting field.

To find out more about the work of the Saracens Sport Foundation and how you can support our work, visit www.saracenssportfoundation.org or call us on 02036 757 243

NORTON ROSE FULBRIGHT

Here at Norton Rose Fulbright we have a great sporting culture coupled with a strong sense of community. As rugby fans, we are delighted to support Wooden Spoon, and help make sure every child can enjoy sport.

We believe in opening up opportunities for every child, and we focus our charitable efforts on supporting young people in our local community in Southwark. As well as providing financial support, we also encourage our people to volunteer at our supported sports clubs, putting their skills to good use with children and young people who are disadvantaged – whether physically, mentally or socially.

We chose to work with Wooden Spoon many years ago, as a charity which shares our values so closely, and I am proud that to this day we are continuing our relationship with this excellent charity.

I wish success and happiness to everyone at Wooden Spoon over the coming year, and I would like to thank everyone involved for their ongoing commitment to disadvantaged and disabled children in the UK.

Peter Martyr
Global Chief Executive
Norton Rose Fulbright

At Artemis, we are deeply aware of our broader responsibility to society and aspire to make a positive difference to the environment and communities in which we work and live. We have been doing so since 2007, when the Artemis Charitable Foundation was founded. Each year the firm gives a proportion of its revenues to the foundation, which manages our charitable activities and our involvement in the wider world. We encourage our people to develop their expertise and professional knowledge, both

through formal training and through self-development. We then encourage them to share their skills through involvement in the various charities and causes we support; such as fundraising, volunteering and visiting the charities at work.

Artemis is delighted to support Wooden Spoon again this year and the work they are doing. This is our eighth year supporting the charity and we believe the opportunities the charity provides are pivotal to transforming the lives of many disadvantaged children. The inspirational values of Wooden Spoon, namely passion, integrity and teamwork, resonate strongly.

From all of us at Artemis, we would like to thank everyone at Wooden Spoon for their dedication and devotion to disadvantaged and disabled children. Thank you.

Wooden Spoon
The children's charity of rugby

CHANGING LIVES

We fund life-changing projects across the UK and Ireland, using the power of rugby to support children with disabilities or facing disadvantage

Wooden Spoon is a registered charity in England and Wales (Reg No: 326691) and in Scotland (Reg No: SC039247)

woodenspoon.org.uk **#helpingkidsthroughrugby**

Wooden Spoon
The children's charity of rugby

WHO WE ARE

Wooden Spoon is the children's charity of rugby, which was founded in 1983. Since then, we have been committed to helping improve the lives of children with disabilities, or facing disadvantage, across the UK and Ireland.

Wooden Spoon believes all children should have access to the same opportunities, no matter what their background. We are extremely proud to say that every penny raised locally in our regions, funds local projects in that area. We are one of the largest UK funders of respite and medical treatment centres, sensory rooms, specialist playgrounds, sports activity areas, and community-based programmes and have so far granted over £28 million to these fantastic projects. Inspired and motivated by our rugby heritage and by working together with the rugby community, with the support of its top sporting heroes, we have been able to help over 1 million children and fund more than 1000 projects.

Our rugby heritage gives us our core values of **passion**, **integrity**, **teamwork** and **fun**. We have over 400 committed volunteers who are raising funds in local communities up and down the country.

Find out more at
woodenspoon.org.uk

THE STORY BEHIND WOODEN SPOON

A wonderful legacy emerged in 1983 after five England rugby supporters went to Dublin to watch England in the final game of the Five Nations Championship against the Irish. The game was lost 25-15 and England finished last in the table with just a single point gained from their draw against Wales.

After the match, in a Dublin bar surrounded by celebrating Ireland supporters, the five England supporters sought some consolation only for three of their Irish friends to present them with a wooden spoon, wrapped in an Irish scarf on a silver platter as a memento of England's dismal season.

Accepting the gift with good humour and grace, the England fans resolved to hold a golf match to see who would have the honour of keeping the wooden spoon.

Just a few months later the golf match was held and in the course of an entertaining day an astonishing sum of £8,450 was raised. The money was used to provide a new minibus for a local special needs school, Park School. This was to be the of first many Wooden Spoon charitable projects that has grown to over 1,000 in the years since. From defeat on the rugby field, and a tongue-in-cheek consolation prize, the Wooden Spoon charity was born.

Our Patron
Our Patron is HRH The Princess Royal who gives generously of her time.

Our Rugby Patrons
The IRFU, RFU, WRU, SRU all support us in our charitable work.

Sporting Partners
We work closely with a variety of clubs, league associations and governing bodies who help us achieve our vision of improving young lives though the power of rugby.

RUGBY FOOTBALL UNION   IRFU   SCOTTISH RUGBY   WRU   PREMIERSHIP RUGBY

Wooden Spoon
The children's charity of rugby

SUPPORTING PROJECTS NEAR YOU

Staff and students at The Usual Place, in Dumfries, have picked up no fewer than 11 awards since the eatery opened its doors for business in 2015.

The sustained success enjoyed by the popular café, which provides citizenship and employment opportunities for young people with additional needs, would not have been possible without Wooden Spoon Scotland's help in firing up its stoves.

The café supports 14 to 26-year-olds in operating the equipment, serving customers, preparing food and also helping to achieve their Scottish Vocational Qualifications and other industry recognised accreditations.

The Usual Place's chief executive officer, Heather Hall, said: "It was really important to have such

a facility because when our young people leave us and move on to work in a hospitality-related environment they will meet the same equipment, utensils and resources they have used here.

"One of the great by-products of the Wooden Spoon Kitchen is it gives our young people the knowledge and understanding to live independently. If they can make a pot of soup or meal in our kitchen, then they can make it in their own home."

The Usual Place is helping to bridge the gap between young people with additional needs, and members of the public. In addition to its culinary commendations, the café is being held up as a model of best practice and blueprint for future projects.

If you would like to apply for a grant or review our qualifying criteria, please visit our website: woodenspoon.org.uk/how-to-apply

Wooden Spoon is a registered charity in England and Wales (Reg No: 326691) and in Scotland (Reg No: SC039247)

     PREMIERSHIP RUGBY

woodenspoon.org.uk
#helpingkidsthroughrugby

FREDDIE'S WEB OF SUPPORT

Freddie, 15, is just one of the estimated 30,000 children born with cerebral palsy in the UK every year. The condition, which affects the brain and causes difficulty with movements, posture and co-ordination, can affect children in many different ways.

But, Freddie is determined not to let this debilitating condition stop him from achieving his dreams of playing football, ideally at The Den, which is home to his beloved Millwall FC.

From being a young child, Freddie's family had been taking him three times a year to a centre 100 miles away for unique and intensive physiotherapy involving a piece of equipment called the 'spider'.

Deanne, Freddie's Mum said: "Freddie was making great progress and it soon became clear that if there was a centre nearer home where he could get more regular treatment it could be transformative."

So Freddie's family and friends came together, fundraised and in 2015 the Freddie Farmer Foundation was born. Wooden Spoon provided a £25,000 donation towards the Spider Therapy suite, which since its opening, has helped over 70 children and young people like Freddie.

The charity's Centre Manager, Karen said: "Our equipment and therapists can have a big impact on a child's confidence. A lot of the people that visit us generally have problems with their balance and worry about falling and hurting themselves, but time at the Centre helps them to have trust in what they are capable of and to reach their full potential."

Freddie, who visits the Centre at least once a week for treatment said: "I work hard with my physio to achieve my goals. We raise the bar all the time so I can achieve my dreams and continually do more and more. I can now stand for small periods at a time and kick a football with my brother and my dream is to play a match with him and win.

"It's so fantastic that not only has the Centre helped me, it has helped so many other children and their families. Physio can be really hard work, but our physios make it fun and the equipment here gives us so much more support. I just wish there were more centres like this for disabled children up and down the country."

To find out how you can support projects helping children like Freddie, visit woodenspoon.org.uk

Wooden Spoon is a registered charity in England and Wales (Reg No: 326691) and in Scotland (Reg No: SC039247)

Registered with **FUNDRAISING REGULATOR**

woodenspoon.org.uk

#helpingkidsthroughrugby

Wooden Spoon
The children's charity of rugby

MAKE A LASTING IMPACT IN YOUR LOCAL COMMUNITY

After providing for your loved ones, please consider leaving a gift in your will to Wooden Spoon.

With your legacy, we can change the lives of children with a disability, or facing disadvantage.

A donation of any size can make such a huge difference to the lives of children with disabilities, or facing disadvantage.

woodenspoon.org.uk/leave-a-legacy

     PREMIERSHIP RUGBY  Registered with FUNDRAISING REGULATOR

RUGBY FOOTBALL UNION IRFU SCOTTISH RUGBY WRU

#helpingkidsthroughrugby

Wooden Spoon is a registered charity in England and Wales (Reg No: 326691) and in Scotland (Reg No: SC039247)

WORLD CUP YEAR
THE BUILD-UP

Heineken Champions Cup
SARACENS POWER THROUGH

by **NEALE HARVEY**

Saracens blitzed their way unbeaten out of a pool containing Glasgow Warriors, Cardiff Blues and Lyon before going into overdrive during the knock-out stages.

Saracens put aside the disappointment of their 2017–18 European campaign by securing a third Heineken Champions Cup title in four years – and in doing so boosted England's World Cup chances immeasurably by providing an in-form core of the squad which headed to Japan. Built on the bedrock of a largely home-produced side containing such Red Rose stalwarts as Owen Farrell, Jamie George, the Vunipola brothers, George Kruis and the indomitable Maro Itoje, Saracens blitzed their way unbeaten out of a pool containing Glasgow Warriors, Cardiff Blues and French newcomers Lyon before going into overdrive during the knock-out stages. Having already been defeated twice by the Men in Black, Glasgow found themselves brushed aside almost contemptuously, by 56–27, when the sides met for a third time in the competition at Allianz Park in late March before Saracens went up a level to dismiss once-mighty Munster 32–16 in their semi-final at Coventry's Ricoh Arena, thus reaching their fourth European final.

After recent Champions Cup excursions to Lyon and Bilbao, tournament organisers EPCR broke new ground once more by taking the seasonal finale to St James's Park, the iconic home of football's Newcastle United. What was billed as a Test showdown, with Saracens fully loaded not only by their England contingent but a host of other international stars such as Wales flyer Liam Williams, Sean Maitland of Scotland and South

Africa prop Vincent Koch, did not disappoint as they took on a Leinster side who might as well have been called Ireland given the galaxy of stars at their disposal.

With Johnny Sexton, Tadgh Furlong, Rob Kearney and Garry Ringrose amongst them, the defending champions were seeking an unprecedented fifth European Cup win, one that would give Irish rugby a fillip ahead of the World Cup after what had been a disappointing Six Nations. And the omens looked promising when, after Sexton's early penalty, Leinster dominated affairs before Furlong battered his way over for a try just after the half-hour mark, converted by Sexton for a 10–0 lead.

You feared for Saracens, who moments before the try had lost Itoje to the sin-bin and both their starting props, Mako Vunipola and Titi Lamositele, to injury. However, like the heavyweight boxer Tyson Fury during his dramatic bout with American Deontay Wilder, Mark McCall's men rose from the canvas, quickly regathered their senses and set about delivering some punches of their own. Farrell slotted a penalty and when Maitland finished a slick backs move on the stroke of half-time for a try that Farrell converted, it was 10–10 and game on. Leinster never recovered.

From appearing so comfortably in control, Leinster were squeezed hard after the break. Farrell put Saracens ahead and when their outstanding number 8, Billy Vunipola, crashed over on 66 minutes for a try, again converted by Farrell, a third Heineken Champions Cup in four years was assured – an achievement that had been founded on the resilience of their England sextet.

It was an important marker, one that Trevor Woodman, England's 2003 World Cup-winning loosehead prop, believed England could capitalise upon in Japan. Woodman, now coaching at Gloucester, opined: 'In 2003, we fed off guys like Martin Johnson, Neil Back and Ben Kay, along with others from Wasps and Gloucester, like Lawrence Dallaglio, Mike Tindall and Phil Vickery – guys who were coming off strong domestic and European campaigns with three successful club sides.

'That confidence increased with what our England team produced and if you look at Saracens now, they're leading the way at home and abroad and setting the standards. They've got the core of England's pack – five of them – plus the captain, Owen Farrell, who's pulling all the strings, and you saw the way they came from behind to win the European and Premiership finals.

'It was the same when we had Johnno as captain; he knew what to do when things got sticky and didn't get carried away. That's the thing I can align between the two sides that gives me the confidence to believe England can win.' By the time this sees print, we'll know if Woodman was right.

Whilst Saracens had dominated Pool 3 on their way to the knock-out stages, the other four groups were nowhere near as clear-cut. Leinster laid down an early Pool 1 marker by thrashing Wasps 52–3 in round one, but were brought down to earth a week later when a revitalised Toulouse defeated them 28–27 at Stade Ernest Wallon, providing a considerable boost for French rugby.

Leinster responded by reeling off four straight wins, including a 29–13 revenge win over Toulouse in round five, but both teams qualified from a pool in which Bath and Wasps managed just one win between them – a poor effort from two sides enduring tough seasons of transition.

Exeter and Gloucester went into Pool 2 with high hopes of progression, with the Chiefs particularly keen to make a mark in Europe. Sadly, their campaign misfired when an opening day 10–10 home draw with Munster and a costly round-two defeat at Castres put them on the back foot. Gloucester, meanwhile, were soundly beaten at Munster and when the two English sides shared a victory apiece when they met in rounds three and four, it enabled Munster to claim top spot.

With Leicester and the Scarlets bombing badly, Pool 4 turned into a shoot-out between French cracks Racing 92 and Ulster. Racing eventually prevailed but Ulster's 26–22 round five victory over the Top 14 side and a dramatic 14–13 win at Leicester on the last day saw them qualify as runners-up – a deserved achievement in what would prove to be the final season for Ireland hero Rory Best.

Edinburgh were heavy odds against in Pool 5, where they were pitted alongside cash-rich French outfits Toulon and Montpellier and a Newcastle side still buzzing from their fourth-placed Premiership finish the previous season. However, guided by the wily ex-England hooker Richard Cockerill, they confounded the bookmakers by thrashing Toulon 40–14 in round two before defeating Newcastle home and away to take charge of the group. A stunning 28–17 win at Toulon set up a final-day showdown with Montpellier – Edinburgh prevailing 19–10 to top their pool.

Home advantage is generally accepted as being key to quarter-final success. On this occasion, though, two away sides would triumph. With two Scottish teams reaching the quarter-finals for the first time, hopes were high that the Champions Cup might head north of the border, with Edinburgh looking the better bet having secured a home tie against a slightly unconvincing Munster.

A record Edinburgh crowd of 36,358 turned up at Murrayfield to witness what the majority hoped would be an imperious march into the semi-finals, but Munster were in no mood to enter into the party spirit and it was their red-clad hordes who went home happy after a 17–13 victory that was built on the doggedness of their pack and embellished by two tries from Keith Earls.

Leinster, without the injured Sexton, overcame Ulster 21–18 in an epic encounter at a sold-out Aviva Stadium thanks to his stand-in, Ross Byrne, who notched two tries and all of his side's points, including a 71st-minute penalty whilst suffering from cramp that broke brave Ulster's hearts. And there was more drama to come, this time in France where Toulouse battled bravely to overcome Racing 92 away from home, 22–21, to set up a shot at reaching their first final since 2010.

Both semi-finals went with the form book, though, with home advantage this time proving crucial. Munster were never seriously in the race at Saracens, whose power game produced six successful penalties from Farrell and tries by Michael Rhodes and Billy Vunipola in a 32–16 victory. Back in Dublin, meanwhile, Toulouse were unable to repeat their quarter-final heroics against Leinster, who triumphed 30–12 courtesy of tries from James Lowe, Luke McGrath and Scott Fardy and 12 points from the boot of fit-again Sexton, with Byrne adding another three-pointer for good measure.

That set-up the Anglo-Irish denouement in Newcastle but in all of this, where was the Welsh challenge? With the Ospreys and Dragons condemned to competing in the Challenge Cup, it had been left to Scarlets and Cardiff Blues to fly the flag for the Principality. Sadly, both crashed out at the pool stage, winning just three of 12 matches between them. A World Cup worry? You might say. But given that Wales managed to complete a Grand Slam and travelled to Japan on a high, what price Champions Cup form? That said, England, via the achievements of their 'double' winning Saracens contingent, would have taken the most pre-World Cup satisfaction.

EUROPEAN CHALLENGE CUP

French giants Clermont Auvergne dominated the European Challenge Cup from start to finish, winning all six pool matches before thrashing Northampton 61–38 in a high-scoring home quarter-final.

Harlequins provided their opposition in the last four but were beaten 32–27 in another entertaining encounter at Stade Marcel-Michelin, leaving Clermont to live-up to their pre-tournament billing as favourites by defeating La Rochelle 36–16 in an all-French final at Newcastle.

The Gallagher Premiership
SARACENS ON TOP AGAIN

by **HUGH GODWIN**

There were dozens of Premiership players whose every performance attracted media comment on whether they were progressing towards a trip to Japan.

Saracens became champions of England for the fifth time, and completed their second league-and-European Cup double to go with the one in 2016, with an astounding comeback to beat Exeter Chiefs 37–34 in the final of the Premiership at Twickenham. The pain felt by Exeter, who have now been beaten three times out of three by their rivals from London in the domestic decider, was epitomised by the sight of their brilliant back Jack Nowell leaving the national stadium on crutches after he wrenched a knee and ankle. It would take from the final date of 1 June all the way to the beginning of October before Nowell played again, for England at the World Cup in Japan.

And the jostling for places in various World Cup squads – not just England's, because the Premiership is of course a cosmopolitan competition – was one of the motifs of a long season which, with next year's final due on 20 June, and the one in 2021 on the 26th, is inexorably eating into the summer space.

Danny Cipriani had moved from Wasps to Gloucester, and the much-discussed fly-half was one of dozens of Premiership players whose every performance attracted media comment on whether they were progressing towards to a trip to Japan. Some such as Faf de Klerk at Sale Sharks and Matt To'omua at Leicester were courted by their countries – South Africa and Australia respectively – with bespoke arrangements under which they flitted between Premiership and international matches in the early months. To'omua and his Leicester and Wallabies team-mate, the hooker Tatafu Polota-Nau, clocked up a staggering number of air miles to do this dual service in September, yet there was no obvious benefit to the Tigers, who were thrashed 40–6 at Exeter on the opening Saturday; the club sacked their head coach Matt O'Connor two days later. O'Connor had in truth been given a stay of execution in the early summer, after the 10-times champions Leicester missed the play-offs in the 2017–18 season, but the savagery of the timing was still a shock.

Leicester installed their backs coach and long-serving former full-back and captain Geordan Murphy as the new boss, and eventually hired the much more widely experienced Mike Ford to work alongside him, but the tunes of glory at Welford Road have been growing fainter by the year. The new forces are Saracens and Exeter – who between them set a storming pace by winning 20 of their 22 league matches up to the end of December – and their nearest challengers were a resurgent Gloucester, whose South African coach Johan Ackermann had revamped his forwards with muscle and nous from his homeland including lock Franco Mostert and flanker Jaco Kriel. Behind them, Cipriani revelled on the front foot and he pulled out no-look passes, daring cross-kicks and a range of lavish scoring plays – often with the benefit of a penalty advantage as insurance – that made him a darling of social-media commentators, newspaper columnists and compilers of TV showreels. Cipriani had, however, also been arrested on a club night out in Jersey in pre-season and his face never fitted with the England coach Eddie Jones as a first- or even second-choice fly-half. Jones did not elucidate his opinion clearly on why, but he let it be known he considered defence as one of Cipriani's shortcomings.

Gloucester had no complaints about their 31-year-old number 10 and by April they were extending Cipriani's contract by another three years as they headed for a third-place finish in the Premiership and qualification for the title play-offs for the first time since

2011. The run ended in a 44–19 loss at Saracens, whose kicking to retain possession was excellent, with Wales's Grand Slam wing Liam Williams prominent, and strength in depth evident when the captain and defensive leader Brad Barritt went off with a hamstring injury, and his replacement Nick Tompkins grabbed a spectacular hat-trick of tries in the opening 17 minutes of the second half.

The other semi-finalists were Northampton, also enjoying a revival under the coaching of Chris Boyd, an apparently avuncular New Zealander whose CV includes work with starry All Blacks such as Beauden Barrett and Ma'a Nonu at the Hurricanes. The England hooker and erstwhile captain Dylan Hartley missed the second half of the season injured, but Northampton relied on a batch of new stars led by flanker Lewis Ludlam and centre Rory Hutchinson – the former went to the World Cup with England; the latter was surprisingly overlooked by Scotland.

Fly-half Dan Biggar made 17 starts for the Saints while assisting Wales's Grand Slammers, and brought direction and drive, while 12 Premiership tries from South Africa scrum-half Cobus Reinach was a staggering return. Ultimately, though, Northampton could be described as the best of the rest, just nipping ahead of Harlequins, Bath and Sale Sharks into the play-offs, where they well beaten by Exeter at Sandy Park.

Finishing in mid-table meant different things to different clubs. Harlequins under Paul Gustard moved in the right direction, while Sale and most notably promoted Bristol in the hands of Pat Lam consolidated their places. Wasps were hampered by injuries, Bath were drifting in the knowledge that head coach Todd Blackadder would be departing at season's end, but the venerable Alan Solomons delivered a decent 10th place for the new owners at Worcester.

Leicester wound up one place off the bottom, saved – is that is the word – by the spectacular fall from grace of Newcastle Falcons. The surprise semi-finalists of the season before were relegated this time around, after struggling through a tough set of opening home fixtures, among which the warning signs were obvious in a series of chances to score tossed away in the 23–22 loss to Wasps. No season swings on one match, and Newcastle ended up 10 points adrift, but the lack of early momentum was crucial, and one sensed that their director of rugby Dean Richards regarded the memorable European Cup wins away to Toulon and home to Montpellier as unhelpful distractions, not inspirations. London Irish were promoted to replace Newcastle as winners of the Championship, with a move to a new stadium shared with Brentford FC set for 2020.

In the background the principal Premiership talking point topic was the sale of 27 per cent of the league's commercial arm to an investment house, CVC Capital Partners, for £200 million, although the 13 shareholder clubs were allowed to increase their share of this vehicle, and reportedly 10 of them did. It was also reported that CVC was to receive an increased share of 45 per cent of revenue above a certain ratchet figure, in an incentive arrangement familiar to any watchers of TV's *Dragons Den*. As CVC was busy striking similar deals around the rugby world, there was a mixture of critical acclaim and disquiet over what new harmonies or upset their involvement may bring. One possibility is that the investors' seat at enough tables might enable them to rationalise or at least renegotiate the complex club and international schedules, including Lions tours.

So to the final of the Premiership almost everyone had predicted, held at a baking-hot Twickenham. Exeter led 7–0 with Australia scrum-half Nic White's try in 26 seconds, and 14–13 after flanker Dave Ewers scored in the 21st minute while Saracens' England lock Maro Itoje was in the sin bin. But as Leinster had found in the European Cup final three weeks previously, it takes more than Saracens being one man down for 10 minutes to beat them, even when that man is the mighty Itoje. The Chiefs were still ahead, 27–23, with a quarter of the match to play – then Saracens unleashed a brilliant team try fashioned by surges from Richard Wigglesworth, Mike Rhodes and England hooker Jamie George up the middle, and finished by the Scotland wing Sean Maitland. With the stricken Nowell withdrawn, the wind was gone from Exeter's sails, leaving the Chiefs' shattered England centre Henry Slade to observe mournfully: 'We had them; we were on top of them. But every time we got near to going two or three scores up they stayed in touching distance.'

Even as Saracens heaved another set of trophies including the A-league Shield and the women's Premier 15s into the display cabinet at Allianz Park, another running story was a Premiership investigation into the club's adherence or otherwise to the league's salary cap. Saracens owner Nigel Wray stated that a set of companies he co-owned with star players such as Owen Farrell and the Vunipola brothers were investments which could rise and fall in value, so they were not salary. There were also newspaper stories of properties used by players and owned by the club. Once the regular season had ended, any penalty applied to Saracens would be carried into the subsequent campaign but still it was a disturbing undercurrent chipping away at the North London side's reputation for decent man-management and fine coaching. They are the successors to Leicester and Wasps from a previous generation in their ability to compete on all fronts, and Wray told one newspaper he would like to see director of rugby Mark McCall replicate Alex Ferguson's dynastical reign at Manchester United and stay for 25 years. McCall has completed 10 years already, and is contracted with his assistants until 2022, but rugby, as with every sport, always retains the capacity to surprise.

Jack Lam of Bristol Bears makes a break during the match with Worcester Warriors at Sixways Stadium, 7 October 2018. Worcester won 52–7, scoring seven tries.

The Guinness PRO14
FIRST SKIRMISHES

by **PAUL BOLTON**

The 2018–19 champions Leinster made an early statement of intent in their pursuit of a hat-trick of titles in 2019–20 and a record seventh overall.

Events in Japan meant that the start of the Gallagher Premiership season in England was pushed back until the Rugby World Cup pool matches had been completed. But in the three other Home Unions the league season spluttered into life in late September. Three rounds of Guinness PRO14 matches had been completed before Scotland had been eliminated from the World Cup by Japan in a low-profile start to the competition.

With most of the competition's leading players in international action on the other side of the world the opening weeks resembled an A-League competition and there was always the risk that the early-season results might be skewed.

Predictably, most sides struggled for consistency with understudies replacing their leading men but Leinster made an early statement of intent in their pursuit of a hat-trick of titles and their seventh overall.

Despite having 14 players on World Cup duty with Ireland – 13 of whom started in last season's PRO14 final – Leinster began their season with three straight wins although they required a hat-trick of tries from Dave Kearney to secure a jittery 32–27 victory over

James Ryan of Leinster on the burst between Matt Fagerson, left, and Callum Gibbins of Glasgow Warriors during Leinster's record sixth title win in the 2019 PRO14 final at Celtic Park in Glasgow. Ryan and his team-mates Sean Cronin (left) and Johnny Sexton were all in Japan with the Ireland squad.

Benetton in Treviso in the opener. Ulster – who provided only three players to Ireland's World Cup squad – Connacht and Munster each suffered an early-season defeat in stuttering starts to the campaign when they were also missing frontline players.

Jack O'Donoghue of Munster is tackled by Owen Jenkins, right, and Jack Dixon of Dragons during Munster's PRO14 Round 1 match win in September 2019.

Ulster also lost the services of tighthead prop Gareth Milasinovich for most of the campaign with a knee injury sustained in pre-season training. Milasinovich was born and raised in South Africa but his grandfather Norman McFarland played for Ulster. Milasinovich was keen to use his ancestry to push his claims for a place in Ireland's squad when he opted to join Ulster from Worcester Warriors but the injury setback means that he will have to wait another month.

Scotland's early exit from the World Cup had a silver lining for Edinburgh and Glasgow – both of whom made faltering starts to the new season – with the early return to club rugby of their international contingents. Glasgow had 16 players on duty in Japan – 12 with Scotland – the most for any PRO14 club apart from Benetton.

Edinburgh walloped Zebre in their opener and then edged out Cardiff Blues at the Arms Park before falling to Leinster at the RDS despite the Irishmen going down to 13 men at one stage. Off the pitch Edinburgh have been given planning permission to develop a 7,800-capacity stadium on the back pitches at Murrayfield which they hope will become their permanent home for the 2020–21 season.

Glasgow, PRO14 runners-up last time round, began their season with a heavy defeat in Bloemfontein by the early pacesetters Cheetahs and then slipped up at home to Scarlets in a cross-pool match. A 17–13 home win against Cardiff Blues belatedly kick-started Glasgow's challenge.

Of the four Welsh regions it was Scarlets who made the best start despite having 11 players with Wales in Japan. Scarlets won their first three matches in Pool B in a successful start under new head coach Wayne Mooar. The former solicitor has swapped Super Rugby, where he worked as the Crusaders' attack coach, for west Wales, where he has succeeded new Wales coach Wayne Pivac. Scarlets' winning sequence included a 54–10 thrashing of Zebre at Parc Y Scarlets, the third straight 50-point beating inflicted on the Italians in a poor start to the season. Even with the early return of 10 players from Italy's disappointing World Cup campaign, Zebre's dismal record in the competition looks set to continue.

Wales's World Cup progress meant that Cardiff Blues supporters had to wait for their first sight of Josh Adams, the wing recruited from Worcester Warriors. Adams, rejected by Scarlets as an academy player, successfully rebuilt his career at Worcester and reluctantly swapped the Gallagher Premiership for the PRO14

to preserve his international place. Adams scored nine tries in his first 18 internationals, including a vital hat-trick in the World Cup victory over Fiji which took Wales into the quarter-finals.

Dean Ryan, another with Worcester connections, has also moved into the PRO14 as Director of Rugby of Dragons, who were the least-affected of the regions with just four players in Wales's World Cup squad. Ryan held a similar position with Worcester before he quit in the summer of 2016. He subsequently joined the RFU as head of international development but resigned earlier in 2019 to join Dragons. An opening-round trip to Thomond Park was a tough assignment for Ryan and Dragons were predictably beaten by Munster. A win against Zebre in Parma followed but Ryan's first home match at Rodney Parade also ended in defeat by Connacht.

Ospreys began their season with consecutive away defeats in Ireland to Ulster and then Leinster, but bounced back to beat Benetton in their first match at the Liberty Stadium where hooker Sam Parry scored a hat-trick of tries in a 24–20 win. Parry's record should have helped to sustain Ospreys while six players, including George North and Wales captain Alun Wyn Jones, were on national duty. However, the knee injury sustained by fly-half Gareth Anscombe in Wales's opening World Cup warm-up match against England has not only ruled him out of the tournament but probably the entire PRO14 season.

The early-season fixture list was kind to Cheetahs, who played their first three matches in Bloemfontein, and they made home advantage count by topping 40 points in each of them, against Glasgow, Ulster and Munster. Repeating those performances against stronger opponents in Europe will be the key to Cheetahs winning Pool A but they seem better equipped to succeed than Southern Kings, the other South African side.

The Kings began the season with Robbi Kempson as interim coach following the departure of Deon Davids during the off-season and virtually a completely new squad with 16 recruits including former Harlequins fly-half Demetri Catrakilis and Jerry Sexton – brother of Johnny – from Greene King IPA Championship side Jersey Reds. Having managed just two wins last season, the Kings began the new campaign with three straight defeats – all of them at home – to Cardiff Blues, Munster and Ulster, and with no players away on World Cup duty there were no excuses for Kempson.

For 12 of the 14 coaches, international calls were disruptive and irritating but the form book from 2015, the last time the start of the competition – then the PRO12 – clashed with the pool stage of the Rugby World Cup, suggested not too much should be read into early-season results.

Four years ago Edinburgh and Scarlets were the only teams to win their first four matches but both ended the season outside the top four, while eventual champions Connacht, runners-up Leinster and beaten semi-finalists Glasgow and Ulster all suffered at least one defeat.

TOP Johnny McNicholl of Scarlets scores his side's seventh try during the Round 2 54–10 victory over Zebre at Parc Y Scarlets.

RIGHT Dan Lydiate of Ospreys claims the line-out during the Round 2 match with Benetton on 12 October. An early red card for Mario Lazzaroni gave Ospreys a crucial advantage.

Under-20 Championship
ANOTHER FRENCH TRIUMPH

by **ALAN LORIMER**

What made France stand above the rest was the experience of seven players from the 2018 winning squad and the overall strength to last the gruelling five rounds of the tournament.

It was France yet again as Les Bluets edged out Australia in the final of World Rugby's Under-20 Championship at the Racecourse Stadium in the Argentinian city of Rosario, becoming only the third country to achieve back-to-back titles and, in the process, sending an encouraging message to their seniors ahead of the Rugby World Cup in Japan.

But you have to feel for runners-up Australia, who, having played hugely attractive and effective rugby throughout the tournament, were pipped in the final by a single point in a 24–23 thriller despite outscoring France by three tries to two.

The closeness of the score in the final reflected the closeness in strength of the top eight countries, each of which looked capable of reaching the semi-finals. Ultimately what made France stand above the rest was the experience of seven quality players from the 2018 winning squad: props Jean-Baptiste Gros and Giorgi Beria, second row Killian Geraci, number 8 Jordan

Fiji winger Epeli Momo rounds an Argentinian tackler during their first-round match. Momo later received a red card and a six-week ban for a dangerous tackle during Fiji's match with New Zealand.

Joseph, fly-half Louis Carbonel, centre Arthur Vincent and wing/full-back Matthis Lebel, and a squad that had the overall strength in depth to last the gruelling five rounds of the championship.

Yet, you might not have bet your *maison* on France early on in the tournament. Les Bluets, after wins over Fiji (36–20), and Wales (32–13), were humbled by hosts Argentina in a 26–47 pleaser for the home crowd. France and Argentina finished level on 11 points at the end of the group stage but under championship rules, if two teams have the same total, then the group winner is decided on the result of the match between the two tied countries. Thus Los Pumitas finished top of Pool A and Les Bluets second, but this was enough to see France into the semi-final as fourth seeds.

France, however, owed much to what unfolded in Pool C where the normal automatic path of New Zealand to the semi-final became blocked after the Junior All Blacks failed by the narrowest of margins to achieve a losing bonus point in their 25–17 defeat to the Baby Boks. That left New Zealand finishing their group with ten points, one below France, and Pool C winners South Africa, who were the only side in the tournament to win all their pool matches, progressing to the semis as top seeds.

England, too, paid the price for not accumulating bonus points, limiting themselves to three tries in their 26–42 loss to Ireland and scoring an identical tally of touchdowns in their 24–23 win over Italy. Not even a substantial 56–33 critic-answering win over Australia in the final Pool B match could save England, who finished with only 9 points – below Ireland (10) and Australia (11).

Ireland's killer blow was their failure to salvage any pool points from their 17–45 defeat to Australia, a sobering scoreline for the Six Nations Under-20 champions. Meanwhile Wales, like England, could amass only 9 pool points, consigning the Welshmen to third place in Pool A despite wins against Argentina (30–25) and Fiji (44–28), counterbalanced, however, by their non-bonus-point loss to France (13–32).

The semi-final draw paired South Africa with France and Argentina with Australia. After so much flamboyant rugby on display in the group stages the match between South Africa and France was a much tighter affair, each side scoring one try apiece, but the pressure exerted by Les Bluets resulted in five penalty goals from the boot of Carbonel to give France a 20–7 win and a place in the final.

Australia were more convincing winners in their semi-final against Argentina. The host nation managed only one try – of the penalty variety – which paled

Second row Joel Kpoku on the charge during England's first-round match with Ireland on 4 June, won 42–26 by Ireland.

Vaughen Isaacs scores South Africa's first try during their 25–17 win over New Zealand at the end of the pool stages. South Africa were the only team with three pool victories.

against the Junior Wallabies' haul of four touchdowns, achieved despite the loss of their abrasive scrum-half Mike McDonald, whose two yellow cards morphed into red. The final scoreline of 34–13 showed the potency and ball-handling skills of the young Australians and for many observers they became favourites to lift the title.

It took the Junior Wallabies only 30 seconds of play in the final to justify that view as wing Mark Nawaqanitawase benefitted from a break by the skilful Isaac Lucas to record the quickest score in a World Under-20 final. Australia then added to their first-half total with a try by hooker Lachlan Lonergan and a penalty from Will Harrison, but with France replying through tries by prop Alex Burin and hooker Theo Lachaud and two penalties and a conversion from Carbonel, Les Bluets led 18–13 at half-time. Then, in the second half, a try from flanker Harry Wilson and the conversion by Harrison gave Australia the lead but two further penalty goals by Carbonel to one by Harrison gave France victory and the World Championship title.

What was so satisfying for France was the way in which they developed throughout the championship and shook off the mixed form they had shown in the 2019 Six Nations Under-20s, when they lost to Ireland in Cork and England at Sandy Park not to mention a scare against Italy before winning 35–31. But like their title team of 2018, the 2019 France side had quality players able to mix a tight game with glorious handling in the wider channels, leading to the conclusion that the form of such as Carbonel, Vincent and Joseph will surely see these players (and others from Les Bluets squad) figuring in the 2023 Rugby World Cup.

For their part Australia had revealed a readiness to challenge for top honours by defeating New Zealand in the Oceania tournament and confirmed their form with some scintillating rugby against Italy and Ireland in which full-back Isaac Lucas, hooker Lachlan Lonergan, skipper and flanker Fraser McReight, centre Semisi Tupou, scrum-half Mike McDonald, flanker Harry Wilson and fly-half Will Harrison announced themselves as future stars.

Meanwhile South Africa gained some consolation for missing out on the final by winning the bronze medal match with a comfortable 41–16 win over Argentina, outscoring the host country 5–2 in the try count.

This was another demonstration of forward power by the Baby Boks, a sizeable number of whom will step up to senior international rugby soon, top predictions being centre Rikus Pretorius, scrum-half Jaden Hendrikse, second rows J. J. van der Mescht and Emile van Herden, and back rows Phendulani Buthelezi and Jaco Labuschagne.

Despite their losses in the final two stages of the championship Argentina must be pleased that they are building a stock of young players who will soon fill the boots of retiring Pumas, scrum-half Gonzalo Garcia, number 8 Juan Bautista Pedemont and fly-half Joaquin Dela Vega Mendia among the bright prospects.

So what of the home nations? England, Wales and Ireland finished 5th, 6th and 8th respectively while Scotland were 12th and thus relegated to the second tier World Under-20 Trophy, the 2020 edition of which will take place next September in Valencia. Scotland thus became the first home nation side to experience the drop, which drives home the point that to survive in this now cut-throat championship, strength in depth and a core of players with professional experience are necessary components.

England might have cause to feel disappointed at finishing fifth after losing only one of their five matches, the Pool B first round defeat to Ireland. But Steve Bates's side finished strongly, reversing the result against Ireland with a 30–23 win and then defeating Wales 45–26 in the fifth place play-off.

Outstanding for England was full-back and tournament top points scorer Josh Hodge, who, aside from his place-kicking skills, showed he has both pace and clever footwork to score tries. Wing Ollie Sleightholme also impressed as did back rows Tom Willis and Aaron Hinkley.

For Wales the tournament gave opportunities for fly-half Cai Evans, wing Ryan Conbeer and hooker Dewi Lake to advance their playing careers, while for Six Nations Under-20 champions Ireland, who lost out to New Zealand in the 7th /8th play-off, the future looks promising for the likes of fly-half Ben Healy, full-back Jake Flannery, centre Stewart Moore and flanker David McCann.

If Scotland's relegation caused a few shockwaves then these were mere ripples compared to the seismic perturbations following the seventh place and lowest-ever finish for New Zealand. Whether this was simply a 'blip' year for the Junior All Blacks, or whether it represents a more permanent change in the world order, remains to be seen.

Elsewhere Italy, Georgia and Fiji can be pleased with their championship campaigns. Italy, who have developed an all-round game, showed up well in 2018 and confirmed that they can compete at this level, notably by running England desperately close. Georgia have more in their armoury than props built like bulldozers while Fiji, given space, can be the consummate entertainers, as they demonstrated in the final round when they ran in nine tries to demolish Scotland with a 59–34 win.

If the 2020 World Rugby Under-20 Championship can reproduce the high standards of the 2019 edition then rugby fans are in for a real treat. And will it be a hat-trick of titles for Les Tricolors? And will New Zealand bounce back? And will newly promoted Japan survive? We shall see.

Vincent Pinto of France hands off Mark Nawaqanitawase of Australia during the tournament final on 22 June. Nawaqanitawase got the first of Australia's three tries; France scored two but Louis Carbonel's kicking saw them home 24–23.

The Six Nations
WALES ALL THE WAY

by **CHRIS JONES**

It was a fitting finale for Warren Gatland, who ended his stellar career in charge of Wales by becoming the first coach to win three Grand Slams in Five/Six Nations history.

This was an incredible 2019 Guinness Six Nations Championship, framed by the looming Rugby World Cup in Japan and acting as a farewell to two of the outstanding coaches of their generation, while one of the greatest players of any age was rightly crowned Player of the Championship.

That man was Alun Wyn Jones whose place in Welsh rugby folklore is now assured after he first lifted the Six Nations trophy alongside his team-mates to celebrate a first Grand Slam since 2012 and then received the individual gong having emerged as the clear winner in a five-man list dominated by Welsh and English players. While Hadleigh Parkes (Wales), Josh Adams (Wales), Liam Williams (Wales), Jonny May (England) and Tom Curry (England) were all worthy contenders it really was a one-horse race.

It was also a fitting finale for Warren Gatland, the Wales head coach, who ended his stellar career in charge of Wales by becoming the first coach to win three Grand Slams in Five/Six Nations history. Gatland has won 43 Six Nations matches, 13 more than any other coach, giving him a wonderful launch pad for the World Cup. Like Jones, Gatland will have a special place in the hearts of Welsh fans.

George North punishes Yoann Huget's error to score Wales's second try in their record Six Nations comeback in Paris.

Joe Schmidt ended his reign as Ireland coach in the Six Nations on a day when his team fell well short of Wales in the final match but he has also made a significant impact on European rugby. The atmosphere

French centre Mathieu Bastareaud challenges Italy's Sergio Parisse during France's 14–25 success in Rome on 16 March.

was incredible in Cardiff and Ireland, the defending champions, were cast in the role of bit players as Wales grabbed the Slam to give themselves the perfect preparation for the World Cup in Japan.

Wales actually started the campaign in less than impressive style and had to produce a historic fight-back from 16–0 down to run out 24–19 winners against France in Paris. Wing George North benefitted from French errors to claim two vital tries on a rain-soaked Friday night. France had stunned everyone – including their own fans – by putting Louis Picamoles and Yoann Huget in for tries as they raced into that 16–0 half-time lead.

At the start of the second half the Welsh revival had the home fans worried as Tomos Williams scored and then Huget lost the ball in his dead ball area and North punished him. Camille Lopez steadied French nerves through the boot, only for Sébastien Vahaamahina to throw a long, floated pass that North picked off to race clear to the line to make it ten wins in a row for the Welsh.

At Murrayfield, Scotland were given a winning start thanks to a Blair Kinghorn hat-trick of tries which did for Italy 33–20. Despite showing signs of attacking improvement this would again be a winless tournament for the Italians whose run of defeats in the Championship would stretch to 22 by the end of the campaign. The loss to Scotland came on the day that Sergio Parisse broke the record for the most appearances in the Championship, overtaking Brian O'Driscoll with 66. Italy came very close to a try bonus-point only for the Scots to steal the ball at the death.

Ireland's title defence collapsed at the first hurdle when Eddie Jones masterminded an England win 32–20 in Dublin, Jonny May, who would finish as top try scorer in the Six Nations with six, got his first just 90 seconds into the match with Henry Slade and Elliot Daly touching down in a 32–20 beating. Cian Healy went over for Ireland, who trailed 17–10 at the break, and while Jonny Sexton's boot suggested a comeback, the Irish were back under their posts when Slade, an increasingly impressive figure in England's midfield, scored. Farrell then added a penalty and England sealed the deal when Slade picked off a Sexton pass for his second try to condemn Schmidt to his first Six Nations defeat at home.

Schmidt was in much better humour after Jacob Stockdale scored a try to help register a 22–13 win over Scotland at Murrayfield. Conor Murray and Keith Earls also grabbed tries as Scotland's hopes of being more than also-rans hit the buffers yet again. Sam Johnson got his first try for Scotland, but there was precious little else for head coach Gregor Townsend to smile about.

Warren Gatland's Welsh team held on for a record-equalling 11th Test win in a row against a competitive Italian side in Rome, triumphing 26–15. Wales made ten changes but led 12–0 thanks to Dan Biggar's boot. However, Braam Steyn scored a try and Tommaso Allan's kicks cut the lead to two points. Gatland was forced to use his bench to ensure a victory that equalled their best run of consecutive wins at Test level. Edoardo Padovani's late try made the count two-all.

England showed how dangerous their backs could be with wing May scoring a marvellous hat-trick in a 44–8 thumping of France at Twickenham to move to the top of the Six Nations table. May's ability to both chase and catch high kicks was impressive as England used the aerial route to produce four first-half tries. Huget and the dangerous Damian Penaud did combine for a first-half try but the French went in 30–8 behind at the break.

A penalty try award by Nigel Owens – refereeing his record 20th Championship match – early in the second half along with a sixth from Owen Farrell made it a day to forget for the French.

The third round of matches saw the French do what the French always do in the Six Nations – they turned things around when seemingly at sixes and sevens. Romain Ntamack scored a try in his first Six Nations start to help his team to a 27–10 win over Scotland in Paris. The son of France star Emile, he was one of four changes made by under-fire head coach Jacques Brunel. Huget and Grégory Alldritt, who scored two tries, ensured a bonus-point victory that left the Scots without a win in Paris since 1999. Ali Price scored a late try for the faltering Scots.

All eyes turned to Cardiff where the match was billed as Grand Slam decider even though we were in the middle of the tournament. Wales were looking for a record 12th consecutive Test victory and England had their sights on a sixth successive Six Nations win over Gatland's men. Lock Cory Hill would become a Welsh national hero with his try in a 21–13 win. England had struck first with Courtney Lawes stealing the ball for Tom Curry to crash over in the 27th minute to score. Wales piled on the pressure and their ball-retention paid off when Hill scored after an amazing 34 phases of play with Biggar's

Josh Adams about to touch down for the second Wales try during Wales's 21–13 victory over England at the Principality Stadium.

conversion taking the lead. Biggar then picked out Josh Adams with a cross kick that saw the wing outjump Elliot Daly to score and send the stadium wild with joy.

Ireland moved themselves right back into contention with a 26–16 win over Italy with Keith Earls and Conor Murray scoring second-half tries on the way to an encouraging bonus-point win in Rome. However, Ireland were still showing inconsistency and Italy came back from nine points down to grab the half-time lead through tries from Edoardo Padovani and Luca Morisi. Ireland saw Keith Earls grab a 29th try for his country as they found a way to pull away from the home side.

Having beaten England, Wales were given a real fright by Scotland before they stayed on course for the Grand Slam with an 18–11 win at Murrayfield. Josh Adams and Jonathan Davies scored first-half tries for 15–6 at half-time. However, Darcy Graham registered his first Test try for the Scots and it took a Gareth Anscombe late penalty to keep Wales on track for glory.

Meanwhile, England bounced back from the disappointment of Cardiff by thumping Italy 57–14 at Twickenham. Two tries each from Manu Tuilagi and Brad Shields, with Jamie George, Jonny May, George Kruis and Dan Robson also crossing, made it a day to forget for Italy. Tommaso Allan and Luca Morisi did give Italian fans something to cheer and the bonus-point win for England left them one point behind Wales going into the final round of games.

ABOVE Sam Johnson of Scotland scores his team's sixth try, giving Scotland the unlikeliest of 38–31 leads in the astonishing Calcutta Cup game.

LEFT Johnny Sexton of Ireland tries to come to terms with Wales's dominance in their last-round encounter.

GUINNESS SIX NATIONS

Wales captain Alun Wyn Jones and his team-mates celebrate with the Championship trophy after their Grand Slam win at the Principality Stadium on 16 March 2019.

The Irish were also in the mix after battling back in the championship following their early failure at home to the English. They outgunned France, whose revival was predictably short-lived, to secure a 26–14 win. France made the scoreline look more competitive with two late tries but this was always going to be Ireland's day. Rory Best, Johnny Sexton and Jack Conan scored tries as Ireland led 19–0 with Earls ensuring the bonus point.

Italy ended yet another campaign without a win as Damian Penaud scored the crucial try in a 25–14 French win while also knocking the ball out of Marco Zanon's hands as he attempted to give his side that elusive victory. Zanon lost the ball with just six minutes remaining – it was that kind of day for head coach Conor O'Shea and his men who saw another try opportunity for Zanon foiled by the post with the ball bouncing clear of the Italian player as he chased a grubber kick.

It was then off to Cardiff where Ireland were attempting to thwart a Welsh Grand Slam party. An animated crowd went mad when Hadleigh Parkes scored after just 70 seconds and Anscombe's boot left Ireland cast in the role of extras as Wales dominated the stage to win 25–7. Anscombe kicked 20 points, having been switched to full-back when George North was injured early in the game. Wales led 16–0 – the same score they had to make up in Paris in the first match of the championship – and it was soon 25–0. Jordan Larmour scored a consolation try for Ireland converted by Jack Carty and then the Grand Slam party really started in Cardiff.

The Welsh triumph made England's final home game of the Six Nations merely an official way of ending the campaign. It turned out to be one of the most amazing matches ever seen in the Championship with Scotland coming back from 31–0 to claim a 38–38 draw that must have had both defence coaches ripping their hair out.

Sam Johnson's late try appeared to have won it for the Scots but up popped George Ford who went over with the final score of a remarkable contest. England ran in four first-half tries through Jack Nowell, Tom Curry, Joe Launchbury and Jonny May with Scotland responding through two from Graham and other tries from Stuart McInally, Magnus Bradbury and Finn Russell.

It was a fitting end to a Six Nations that proved once again why it is the most game's most fantastic championship.

Southern Championship
SPRINGBOKS TAKE THE TITLE

by RAECHELLE INMAN

It was the first title for the Boks since the inception of the Rugby Championship, and their first southern hemisphere title since winning the Tri-Nations in 2009.

Hope is important. It's what defines us as human beings. The Rugby Championship left the rugby world with hope and real expectations that the 2019 World Cup in Japan would be an open race. The All Blacks were three-time back-to-back defending champions entering this year's Championship, and have consistently dominated the tournament. But this time showed that if a team takes the fight to the Kiwis, they can be defeated. And they were. And we all cheered. Maybe the 2019 World Cup wasn't a foregone conclusion?

It was the eighth season of the annual southern hemisphere Rugby Championship in 2019. The Championship is a contest for southern hemisphere rugby supremacy, comprising Argentina, Australia, South Africa and New Zealand. The competition is operated by SANZAAR, a joint venture of the four countries' national unions.

Due to the World Cup, the 2019 Rugby Championship competition was shortened to three rounds, rather than the usual six. The World Cup, in conjunction with

Herschel Jantjies of the Springboks during the opening weekend of the Rugby Championship, in action against Australia at Emirates Airline Park in Johannesburg, 20 July 2019.

All Black full-back Ben Smith tries to swerve past Matias Orlando of the Pumas during the opening round of the Championship, at Jose Amalfitani Stadium in Buenos Aires.

the absence of the June Tests due to the unbroken Super Rugby season, also saw the Championship brought forward in timing.

Whilst we all know that anything can, and does, happen over the endurance of a World Cup, this precursor event was a good test of the pecking order of the southern hemisphere nations as they stood – right on the eve of the Cup. And through the lens of this Australian writer, who has somewhat lost faith in rugby union as a code and the Wallabies' ability to compete internationally, the shock Australian win over the All Blacks 47–26 on 10 August in Perth restored a glimmer of hope that the future is not pre-determined.

The opening match of the 2019 Rugby Championship started out predictably with the Wallabies travelling to Ellis Park in Johannesburg to face the Springboks on 20 July.

Neither country troubled the Super Rugby final with a team, so this Test match was played at frenetic speed – both countries had something to prove. Australia struggled on the high veld with the home side dominating, running in five tries to the Wallabies two.

In a contest where both sides had a player in the sin bin, Springbok half-back Herschel Jantjies had an electric debut, scoring twice and playing a role in setting up Lood de Jager's 24th-minute try. South Africa ran in convincing winners 35–17.

After New Zealand's Crusaders beat the Jaguares 19–3 to win their tenth Super Rugby title on 6 July, Argentina hosted the All Blacks two weeks later. This round one Rugby Championship game was a much closer affair than anticipated but New Zealand held on to take a narrow victory 20–16 in Buenos Aires.

It was one of the Pumas' best chances in history to take the scalp of the Kiwis and achieve a famous victory. But New Zealand's trademark attributes of strong defence, sheer grit and making the most of limited opportunities proved to be successful. The Pumas managed to keep the All Blacks scoreless in the second half, but it wasn't enough. It was a heart-breaking defeat for Mario Ledesma's side, who dominated much of the contest.

Round two opened on 27 July with another close encounter when Argentina took on the Wallabies in Brisbane. Fresh from round-one losses this was a chance to reinstate some pride for Australia, and for the Pumas to attempt to get a win under their belt.

Five-eighth Christian Lealiifano was solid for the home side, kicking 11 of the Wallabies' 16 points and also playing a hand in winger Reece Hodge's try late in the first half. The Wallabies led 10–3 at the break.

In the second period Los Pumas squandered several try-scoring opportunities before finally crossing with six minutes to play.

In a scrappy match, strewn with handling errors, the Wallabies managed to secure a solid, but not spectacular, 16–10 win. The Pumas had fought with everything in both matches.

Playing a Test match in New Zealand is never easy. When the Springboks lined up in Wellington 23-year-old Herschel Jantjies was ready to build on his debut the prior week to make his mark off the bench against the World Champions.

The All Blacks trialled an intriguing positional switch by playing regular five-eighth Beauden Barrett at full-back and Richie Mo'unga in the number 10 jersey.

After being dominated for most of the first half, New Zealand broke through with Beauden Barrett setting up centre Jack Goodhue's first-half try and kicking the conversion which gave the All Blacks a flattering 7–6 half-time lead. Springbok fly-half Handré Pollard kicked all of the Springboks' points to keep them in the game.

In a battle of attrition, the All Blacks shifted focus after the break, holding the ball and continuing to build pressure to take more control in the second half. Barrett and Mo'unga added three penalties to one by Pollard but the All Blacks paid for a lack of concentration as South Africa found late resolve. Reserve half-back Jantjies was the hero for the visitors at the end of the encounter, latching on to a Cheslin Kolbe chip and juggling before crossing the try line with 50 seconds remaining. Pollard slotted the pressure conversion to cement the third draw in the history books between the great rivals.

A 16-all draw with the All Blacks was a clear confirmation that the Boks were a force to be respected. There was a feeling the mighty All Blacks could be matched and on 10 August a big upset followed in front of a record crowd for a sporting event in Western Australia.

The Wallabies stunned World Champions New Zealand with an inspired 47–26 Test win in Perth. The All Blacks are not used to losing so it must have come as a surprise to Kiwi rugby fans when the Wallabies romped to victory. Michael Cheika's men scored six tries to four. The Australians had gone into the game with little chance of knocking over their arch-rivals, but delivered their best performance in years to make a statement ahead of the World Cup.

But it was controversial. French referee Jérôme Garcès sent New Zealand's Scott Barrett off with a red card on the stroke of half-time for a shoulder charge that clipped Wallabies captain Michael Hooper in the head, reducing the All Blacks to 14 players for the remainder of the match. It was a tough call, and the Kiwis claimed Barrett was treated unfairly. They suggested that a yellow card, and 10 minutes in the sin bin, would have been a far more appropriate punishment for the second-rower.

Playing with 14 men for an entire half was always going to be a battle, even for the All Blacks. But in reality, Australia already had their tails up after a dominant first half and took a 16–12 lead into the break. They went on to take full advantage of the situation, scoring the most points ever against New Zealand and equalling the record for the biggest winning margin (21 points) against the All Blacks.

It was difficult to pick the Wallabies' best with Hooper everywhere, half-back Nic White had an outstanding game and the Wallabies forwards dominated. James O'Connor, who started his first match for the Wallabies in six years, booked his ticket to Japan as he set up a try and gave the attack plenty of options.

Sam Whitelock takes on Malcolm Marx (2) and Franco Mostert during the 16–16 second-round Rugby Championship Test at Westpac Stadium in Wellington.

The Wallabies had extended the margin to 26–12 early in the second half with giant flanker Lukhan Salakaia-Loto scoring before centre Samu Kerevi set up another. The bustling centre ran over the top of Beauden Barrett before off-loading to White. Barrett exacted some revenge six minutes later when he darted through flimsy Wallabies defence, with the conversion closing the gap to seven points.

That was as close as the undermanned Kiwis could get as the scoreboard ticked over for Australia. Reece Hodge scored his second try while fellow winger Marika Koroibete, who was dangerous all night, also crossed the line. Full-back Kurtley Beale's 80th-minute angled run from close range was a glorious sixth try for the home side.

To cap the most open tournament in years, South Africa clinched the Rugby Championship title with a thumping win over Argentina in sunny Salta. It was the first title for the Boks since the inception of the Rugby Championship, and their first southern hemisphere title since winning the Tri-Nations in 2009.

Their 25-year-old fly-half Handré Pollard played the match of his career, scoring two of his side's five tries and kicking five penalties and three conversions for a personal haul of 31 points, his best tally in an international.

Argentina's winger Santiago Cordero had shocked the South Africans by going over in the corner in the second minute of the game but hooker Mbongeni Mbonambi put the visitors 8–7 ahead after a driving maul 13 minutes in.

Pollard and Puma fly-half Nicolás Sánchez then got locked into a kicking duel, exchanging penalties, before the 25-year-old South African dived over the try line just before the break to make it 24–13.

The Springboks' progress slowed early in the second half when scrum-half Faf de Klerk was sin-binned, only for Pollard to cross again.

Pollard also assisted for winger Makazole Mapimpi's score in the 64th minute to cap off a virtuoso Test performance. The other South African winger, Cheslin Kolbe, added another try in the 67th minute to extend the winning score line to an eventual impressive 46–13 win.

Coach Rassie Erasmus was delighted with the all-round team effort, especially the muscle of the forwards, who were the dominant pack, wreaking havoc in the scrum.

This triumph gave the unbeaten Springboks a bonus point and a total of 12 points from their three matches in the Rugby Championship, four more than second-placed Australia.

While there were just three rounds of Rugby Championship rugby, there was a fourth weekend of rugby involving the same four nations. South Africa and Argentina met in a Rugby World cup warm-up match with the Boks defeating the Pumas 24–18 in an arm-wrestle at Loftus Versfeld, Pretoria.

The Bledisloe Cup was decided this year by two games, a home-and-away series, with the second game after the end of the shortened Rugby Championship. New Zealand and Australia played this match at Eden Park, Auckland, with Australia leading the series 1–0.

But the Wallabies' sweet victory was short-lived, with the All Blacks gaining revenge for the prior weekend's drubbing in Perth. New Zealand held the Wallabies scoreless 36–0 at the Eden Park fortress, where the Wallabies haven't won since 1986. The five-try thrashing continued New Zealand's 16-year stranglehold over their Trans-Tasman rivals in the Bledisloe Cup.

The Rugby Championship proved that South Africa's game has moved beyond a reliance on big, bullying forwards as they now have some handy backs and, as always, a reliable goal kicker. The Wallabies remain inconsistent; on their day they can beat anyone, but they are dependent on scoring tries, as they don't have a reliable kicker, which proves costly again and again in internationals. The best hope that any team has to beat the mighty All Blacks is for the team to have their best possible game and the New Zealand side to have an uncharacteristic off-day. That's realistically the only combination that will lead to a giant-slaying victory.

The results of the Rugby Championship provided a level of promise to the rugby world about what might just be. It seems the All Blacks kept a few tricks up their sleeve during the Championship, not revealing too many of their planned strategies and try-scoring moves prior to a World Cup. But no side, especially the All Blacks, likes to be beaten. The psychological blow was short-lived and equilibrium was reinstated to the natural order of things with the demolition of the Wallabies at Eden Park. This signalled, not surprisingly, that New Zealand rugby was peaking again just in time for their quest to secure the William Webb Ellis trophy for the third tournament in succession.

But South Africa's draw with, and Australia's win over, the All Blacks combined with the valiant efforts of the Pumas gave non-Kiwi rugby fans a ray of hope for what might unfold in Japan.

Contrasting fortunes. **ABOVE RIGHT** Reece Hodge of the Wallabies scored a pair of tries to help Australia to their record win over the All Blacks in the first Bledisloe Cup match.

RIGHT A try from Sonny Bill Williams helps the All Blacks get their revenge at Eden Park in Auckland a week later.

The Warm-Up Games
READY FOR REAL BATTLES?

by **PAUL BOLTON**

Coaches took the opportunity to try different combinations and fill in the last gaps in their squads for Japan, but the intensity of real competition was seldom seen.

It was the phoney war before the first shots were fired. A month of warm-up matches – some between familiar foes – gave coaches the opportunity to experiment with different combinations and offered players a last chance to stake their claim for Rugby World Cup squad places. Predictably the matches lacked the intensity and competitive element of the Six Nations when championship points are at stake and were less meaningful than autumn internationals when the best of the northern and southern hemispheres are pitted against each other.

In the main the matches merely reinforced what was already known about most of the teams. England are a force to be reckoned with at Twickenham, Wales enjoy playing England in Cardiff, Scotland and France are infuriatingly unpredictable, Ireland are not the power they were a year ago and Italy continue to struggle to land a blow at the highest level.

England began their build-up to Japan by ending Wales's 14-match unbeaten run with a 33–19 victory on a Sunday at Twickenham. England gave debuts to Willi Heinz, Lewis Ludlam, Joe Marchant and Jack Singleton,

Luke Cowan-Dickie of England celebrates his try during the England v. Wales warm-up at Twickenham.

while Wales lost fly-half Gareth Anscombe with a knee injury which ruled him out of the World Cup. A maiden international try from Exeter hooker Luke Cowan-Dickie helped to deny Wales their first win at Twickenham since 2015.

Wales gained revenge with a 13–6 victory over England at the Principality Stadium six days later, a victory that took them to the top of the world rankings for the first time and knocked the All Blacks off top spot after a reign that had lasted ten years. The only try was scored by George North, who latched on to a crossfield kick from Dan Biggar, who filled the gap left at fly-half by Anscombe's misfortune.

England bounced back spectacularly the following week when they recorded a record win over Ireland – 57–15 – at Twickenham and scored eight tries in an emphatic and outstanding team performance. Wing Joe Cokanasiga scored England's first try and brought up their half-century with his second against a subdued Ireland, who missed the opportunity to displace Wales at the top of the world rankings.

England failed to hit those heights in their final warm-up match against Italy when they staged an international in Newcastle for the first time. A crowd of more than 50,000 in the football-mad north-east suggested that the initiative was a success but England were efficient rather than effervescent, scoring all four of their tries in the second half.

Wales failed to build on their home win over England and left for Japan with back-to-back defeats by Ireland – 22–17 in Cardiff in Warren

ABOVE England lock Joe Launchbury is tackled by Wales flanker James Davies and lock Jake Ball during the Cardiff warm-up game.

RIGHT Coaches Joe Schmidt (L) and Warren Gatland in conversation before the first of their two warm-up meetings, in Cardiff.

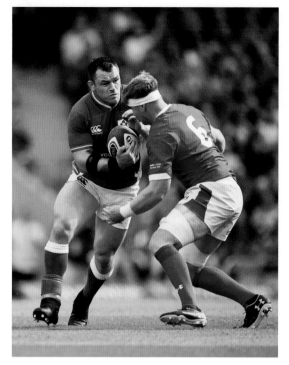

ABOVE Aaron Wainwright of Wales and Cian Healy of Ireland during the second warm-up game between their teams. Both went to Japan.

ABOVE RIGHT One of the unlucky ones: Sam Skinner wins a line-out for Scotland v. France, but a hamstring injury later in the match ruled him out of the World Cup.

Gatland's last Test in charge on home soil and 19–10 in Dublin. A try from wing Owen Lane on debut was the highlight of the first meeting in Cardiff. A week later Wales failed to convert territory and pressure into points and were beaten by tries from Tadhg Furlong and James Ryan.

Ireland began their preparations with a hard-earned 29–10 victory over Italy in Dublin. Joe Schmidt fielded an experimental XV with places in the World Cup squad up for grabs and twice trailed to a lively Italian side, before Ireland, with Chris Farrell impressive in defence, pulled away; Dave Kearney, Andrew Conway, Jordi Murphy and Kieran Marmion scored tries.

Scotland did not play any of the other Home Unions with head coach Gregor Townsend preferring two matches against France – each won by the home side – followed by back-to-back encounters with Georgia. France ran out 32–3 winners in Nice where Maxime Médard scored a brace of tries. Scotland managed to shore up their defence for the return match and, despite conceding an early try, they secured a 17–14 win with a second-half touchdown from Chris Harris.

Against Georgia Scotland won 44–10 in Tbilisi – they were the first Tier One nation to play in Georgia – in sultry conditions which Townsend hoped would replicate those his players were expected to face in Japan. A 36–9 win at Murrayfield in the return was Scotland's 300th in internationals. The win in Tbilisi was also Scotland's first away from Murrayfield in a year and featured maiden tries from Rory Hutchinson (two), Scott Cummings and Ben Toolis. At Murrayfield, Scotland scored 19 points in seven minutes in the final quarter and denied the visiting team a try for the first time in more than two years.

Georgia's other warm-up match was a 24–20 home victory over South African side Southern Kings, who were preparing for the PRO14 season.

Italy's warm-ups included a confidence-building 85–15 win over Russia in San Benedetto del Tronto but they left for Japan having suffered two successive defeats, going down 47–19 to France in Paris the week before they were beaten by England. Full-back Matteo Minozzi scored a hat-trick of tries in the victory over Russia but the margin of Italy's victory was counter-

ABOVE RIGHT As so often before, Sergio Parisse wins line-out ball for Italy, but in a losing cause, during their defeat by France in Paris.

RIGHT Johnny Gray on the charge for Scotland during the Murrayfield leg of their two-match encounter with Georgia.

balanced by the fact that Russia suffered embarrassing home defeats to Jersey Reds, from the Greene King IPA Championship, and Connacht in subsequent warm-up matches.

The phoney war was over and the real battles would be played out in Japan.

Developing Nations
OUTSIDERS AND ALSO RANS

by **CHRIS THAU**

The matches in the pool stage in Japan have confirmed that the participating unions are on the right track, though their progress is uneven and irregular.

A two-speed World Cup is a reality World Rugby must face and deal with. There are teams that battle for the trophy and teams for whom finishing third in their pool and therefore securing a starting slot in the next RWC tournament is a more modest yet achievable objective. There are also participants for whom reaching the RWC final tournament is in itself a considerable achievement. So far, since the tournament kicked off in New Zealand in 1987, only four nations – New Zealand, South Africa, Australia and England – have had their names engraved on the plinth of the Web Ellis trophy, with a fifth (France) reaching the final stage on three occasions; Argentina, Scotland and Wales have reached the semi-finals at different times in various tournaments. There is not much of a difference this time either.

Before the ninth RWC tournament kicked off in Tokyo I visited my local betting shop in search of the bookmaker's view on who was going to be the 2019 RWC Champions. Unsurprisingly the three top bets were New Zealand at 11/8, England 4/1, and South Africa 9/2, followed by Ireland 9/1, Wales 12/1, Australia 16/1. For

> Philip Mack of Canada during the repechage World Cup qualifying match with Hong Kong in November 2018 in Marseille. Canada won 27–10 to gain the last available place in the main tournament.

Florin Vlaicu of Romania sets his line going during the Rugby Europe Championship match with Georgia at Cluj Arena in February 2019. Georgia won 18–9; Vlaicu kicked Romania's three penalties.

nearly one-third of the participants, that is Canada, Tonga, Namibia, USA, Uruguay and Russia, the odds at 1,000/1 were either dismissively low or exceedingly generous, depending which side of the bookmaker's till one stood. The next three Georgia, Italy and Samoa were bracketed in the 500/1 category while Japan, then 11th in the odds list, were given the benefit of the doubt for their 2015 exploits against South Africa and Tonga and listed with a modestly generous 250/1. Fiji, who were fielding what the pundits called the best-prepared and selected team in their RWC history, shared the 250/1 odds with Japan, while Scotland, on the strength of their 80/1 odds, were 9th in the list and therefore unlikely to get past the quarter-finals. Given the very physical, at times brutal nature of the game, this hierarchy is unlikely to change, despite the gallant challenges of the likes of Uruguay, Tonga, Russia, Namibia and Fiji, to mention just a few, and in fact illustrates the chief weakness of the RWC format in the professional age.

Among the 20 nations competing in Japan, only four or five arrived ready to challenge for the Webb Ellis Cup with the other 15/16 providing a colourful and dynamic rugby background to the main cast. Add to those the three or four teams who had narrowly failed to qualify, or had the potential to reach the last 20 and then one has a fair hierarchy of the worldwide game – 24 rugby nations warts and all. Is it enough for a heroic Namibia to be in contention (10–9) with the All Blacks for 30 minutes and to end up walloped 71–9? Despite the bravery of the Namibians this kind of outcome does not confer on the RWC tournament the credibility it is craving for. And this is valid for the gutsy Russians, the gallant Teros, and the fearless Canadians. It is the format of the RWC, basically unchanged from 1987, that is at fault, and in order to overcome this a change of structure, with a premier division of 12 teams, operating on a promotion–relegation basis with a 2nd division of 12, could provide a solution and help the tournament win the credibility it strives for.

So far only Argentina, who impressed in 1999 by reaching the quarter-finals and finished in bronze medal position in 2007, and Japan, thanks to their spectacular defeat of South Africa in Brighton in 2015, confirmed and upgraded by their impressive feats of 2019, when they put Ireland and Scotland to the sword, seem to have broken the mould. As the Cherry Blossoms' head coach, former NZ skipper and Hurricanes' coach Jamie Joseph pointed out, Japan have been preparing the Irish ambush for some time, which is not surprising, knowing the Japanese propensity for hard work and mimetic expression in sport. One could argue that their march towards

Sandro Todua of Georgia is tackled by Lucas Levy of Spain during the 2019 Rugby Europe Championship. Georgia won the match 24–10 and eventually completed a Grand Slam; Spain finished second in the table.

rugby respectability commenced on 4 June 1995 when New Zealand inflicted on a distraught Japanese team a humiliating 145–17 defeat, still the most one-sided match in RWC history. Twenty years later, they confirmed that the world of rugby had turned on its head, when they beat South Africa 34–32 in Brighton. However, unlike the 2015 RWC, when their defeat of South Africa came out of the blue, though Eddie Jones and his lieutenants may claim differently, in 2019 Joe Schmidt and his Irishmen had been forewarned, regardless of whether Ireland fielded their best fifteen or not. The fascinating aspect of Japan's progress might not necessarily be their success on the field of play, though that has played a significant part in the recognition process. It is the stunning quality of their game, the pace, the vision and the accuracy of their passing, the solidity of their set-pieces, the amazingly high rhythm in attack and their patience and discipline in defence that make one wonder. So it is possible! It takes time, as Jamie Joseph has said, and add to that patience, ambition as well expertise and one may have a winning formula. But still that is not enough.

Japan and Argentina are the most noticeable products of this quiet rugby revolution, which has been taking place since the beginning of the century. The matches in the pool stage in Japan have confirmed that the participating unions are on the right track, though their progress is uneven and irregular, as shown by the plucky Russians in their defeat by Ireland, by Tonga in their gallant challenge of both Argentina and France, with the latter lucky to escape defeat by two very narrow points, Uruguay's mighty effort against both Fiji and Australia, by Canada's stubborn and fearless defence against the All Blacks, by Namibia's amazing efforts against the World Champions or the US Eagles' brave challenge against France. Those nations can play, in patches, quality football, yet they are short of that consistency, both physical and mental, and the experience required for 80 minutes of unswerving effort and ultimately success. Their halting progress has been more or less made possible by the emergence of an international squad of high-quality coaches, sponsored by World Rugby, who are working full time to bring them up to the required standard: Milton Haig in Georgia, Toutai Kefu in Tonga, Canada's Kingsley Jones, Esteban Meneses and Craig White in Uruguay, Gary Gold with the US Eagles, Phil Davies in Namibia, Steve Jackson in Samoa, John McKee in Fiji, and Lyn Jones in Russia. Add to that resources and a credible competition format and they could turn RWC into the most exciting and admired competition in the world of sport.

With an eye to the future, the Canadian Union has taken the unusual step to appoint, even before the end of the RWC, head coach Kingsley Jones as High Performance Director of the men's teams, having previously enlisted the former New Zealand RWC-winning coach Graham Henry in an advisory role. 'It's

Antoine Koffie of Italy is tackled by Josh Nasser of Australia during the 2019 World Rugby Under-20 Championship in Argentina. Italy's age group teams have clearly improvedl in recent times.

exciting to see Rugby Canada taking the necessary steps to set Canada in the right direction, and I'm humbled and honoured to be a part of it,' said Jones, who coached Russia in the 2011 RWC. 'There's huge potential ahead of us with the focus on a developing pathway through the Pacific Pride Academy, the growth of Major League Rugby, the men's and women's Olympic qualification, and changes to the player-release window. These all stand to be a huge boost for Canadian rugby, and will position us well for the 2023 Rugby World Cup and beyond.' This is a model that should be emulated.

Both Romania and Spain, dumped out of the 2109 RWC for a series of eligibility issues, have commenced work with the 2023 RWC in mind. Spain coach Santiago Santos Muñoz has already selected a young and promising squad that should form the backbone of the new team for the campaign in the 2020 Rugby Europe Championship, the elite continental competition, the launch-pad for the 2023 campaign. Spain, coached at the time by their current president Alfonso Feijoo, qualified for the main RWC tournament in 1999, so far their only appearance in the finals. Romania, who missed the 2019 RWC for the first time in their history, are determined to re-enter the race, under new management. The interim head coach Marius Tincu, a former international hooker who played for Perpignan in France, has been made head of the High Performance Department and Director of Rugby as the Romanian Federation announced the appointment of former England and Scotland coach Andy Robinson as the new head coach of the Oaks. Robinson will meet Tincu and the Romanian Federation officials in November, as he will commence the preparations for the new international season in the aftermath of the RWC. 'My main purpose is to help the country to qualify for the 2023 RWC in France … and I believe this is an achievable objective,' Robinson said. Germany, who reached the final repechage stage of the 2019 RWC with Mike Ford as head coach, will try to go one better, under their new head coach Mark Kuhlman, a former international player and coach. Finally, the former Uruguay captain and head coach Pablo Lemoine, who briefly took control of the German team last season, is now in charge of the Chile selection, another South American developing nation hoping to reach the RWC finals for the first time in 2023.

From Taiso to Bushido
RUGBY IN JAPAN

by **CHRIS THAU**

It was clear from the outset that the Japanese students took to the game like ducks to water. They were fascinated by its complexity and rituals, as well as by its physicality.

Modern Japanese sport, including rugby, is the by-product of the political and cultural modernisation process, generally described as the Meiji Restoration, that radically changed the fabric of Japanese society during the reign of the Emperor Meiji between 1868 and 1912 It was triggered off by the arrival of a US naval mission led by Commander Matthew Perry in 1853 (during the Edo Period), which led to the demise of the Japanese Shogunate, while opening five ports to trade with the West. It was the period when the term *taiso* or *taijutsu*, 'the art of body exercise', was coined by Japanese educationalist and philosopher Nishi Amane, which helped create the framework for the development of a national policy in which physical education and sports played an increasingly significant role.

During the early decades of the Meiji Period, football matches of uncertain nature between the crews of visiting British ships and the Western residents of the open Japanese ports became a relatively common occurrence. According to Mike Galbraith, an Old Rugbeian who researched the history of Yokohama Football Club, the first club to play rugby in Japan and Asia was Yokohama C&AC in 1874 when a drawing in the *Graphic* magazine depicted a football match between the club and a visiting team, most likely the crew of one of the many British ships anchored in the harbour. Kobe also became an open port at the end of the Edo Period and a sports club was founded by one Alexander Cameron Sim, a chemist of Scottish stock, in 1870. The history of the Kobe club also mentions a Mr Outbridge, a graduate of New Brunswick's Mount Allison University, as the founder of the rugby section, with an early rugby match against a crew of sailors recorded in 1876.

Alas, one must hasten to add, those matches had little or no effect on the native Japanese population, yet to be exposed to the games and sporting pastimes of Victorian Britain. The only sport that had an immediate impact on Japanese youth was American baseball, introduced by Horace Wilson, a teacher at Kaisei School in Tokyo in 1872; baseball has become and remains the most popular sport in Japan.

On the rugby front, the proximity of the Yokohama club to Keio University has played a significant role in the birth of Japanese rugby and a stone column in a bush-growth on the University playing fields marks the

place where the history of Japanese rugby commenced at the start of the 20th century. Former Kobe Steel club scrum-half Shinichi Tanaka, the great-grandson of Ginnosuke Tanaka, one of the founders of Japanese rugby and the first President of the Japan Rugby Union, explained the circumstances that led to rugby becoming one of the leading varsity games in Japan, and the country eventually the host of RWC 2019.

The 1874 illustration of an all-European rugby match at Yokohama, watched by a few locals.

Towards the end of the 19th century, Ginnosuke Tanaka, a graduate of Keio University, went to Cambridge University in England, where he met the son of a Yokohama baker and fellow Keio graduate, Edward Bramwell Clarke. During their time at Cambridge, the two shared an interest in rugby football and once they returned to Japan in 1899 they decided to teach the Japanese students the rudiments of the new game. Clarke took a leading role especially since on his return to Japan he was offered a teaching position at Keio University. It took a while for their coaching to bear fruit, yet it was clear from the outset that the disciplined Japanese students took to the game like ducks to water. They were fascinated by its complexity and rituals, as well as by its physicality. In about a year the Keio youngsters managed to master the basic skills of the game, which enabled the University team to take on the expatriates of the Yokohama Club. It was 1901 and this was the first match involving Japanese players in the country.

There is not much known about the match, other than that the students provided a gallant challenge to their more experienced opponents, losing 35–5. What is, however, known and has entered the annals of history is the line-up of the team with Tanaka at half-back and Edward Clarke at full-back: (*from 1 to 15*) Shunjiro Mori, Fujio Yamazuki, Masao Matsuoka, Kiroku Fukuzawa, Yoshio Yoshitake, Kazuichi Ogura, Seizo Hamada, Ichinosuke Suzuki, Ginnosuke Tanaka, Heihachiro Kaieda, Kenjiro Shiota, Shiro Suzuki, Ichiro Hirano, Jinnosuke Sano and Edward B. Clarke; Keio University points came from try-scorer Shiota and Clarke who converted it.

Coincidentally or not, these were the days when an abridged version of the novel *Tom Brown's School Days* by Thomas Hughes was published in Japan, followed by translations by Tsukumatsu Okamoto and Tomomasu Muryama in 1903 and 1904. Japanese historians describe the novel as the most popular English-language textbook in Japanese colleges and high schools at the time. This was followed in 1909 by the translation of the Laws of the Game into Japanese, a major undertaking that enabled the slow, but determined and well-charted progress of Rugby Football – called by Japanese media 'Ra-style' football, in an effort to differentiate it from Association Football called 'A-style' football – in its most fertile ground, the Japanese schools and colleges. While the role played by Thomas

TOP Shinichi Tanaka and the monument commemorating the 1901 match between Keio University and the Yokohama club.

TOP RIGHT The Keio University team for that game, with Edward Clarke and Ginnosuke Tanaka in the centre of the group.

RIGHT Prince Chichibu welcomes the 1932 Canada team. Records are uncertain but Japan probably won the Test 38–5.

The Brighton moment. Karne Hesketh of Japan scores the winning try against South Africa, RWC 2015.

Hughes's novel in the evolution of the Japanese rugby has yet to be quantified, there is very little doubt that rugby in its pure form had a profound, long-term impact on Japanese sport and society.

E. B. Clarke went on teaching English and coaching rugby at Keio until 1910 when he was forced to give up the role following an accident. However, while Clarke and Tanaka were united in their desire to make the Japanese students sample the joy of rugby, their philosophies were quite different, an aspect which, in long term, secured the success of rugby as the main winter sport of Japanese academia and eventually the country. Interestingly, Clarke the European, viewed the game as an enjoyable pastime eminently suited for the sport-deprived Japanese youngsters of his era. Tanaka, the keeper of Japanese traditions, on the other hand, viewed rugby in a more ethical context, very much in line with the prevalent *bushido* philosophy of the samurai warrior. The difference between their approaches, observed Tanaka's great-grandson Shinichi Tanaka, himself a former coach of Keio University, has been to an extent responsible for the elevated position of the new game in Japanese society.

'As Professor Clarke wrote, Japan has got four distinct seasons, a wonderful autumn in particular, and Japanese students of the time did not do much sport. So he felt that by teaching them rugby he would offer them a great pastime,' said Tanaka Junior. 'It is said that my great-grandfather worked so hard to popularise rugby in Japan because during his time at Cambridge University he got really fascinated by rugby football and its ethical standards, while deriving so much pleasure from playing it.'

'The two teamed up in order to teach Japanese youngsters the game of rugby. However, I believe that at the root of my great-grandfather's effort was more than just simply teaching rugby. It was also the desire to pass on to future generations the elements that make rugby special. Consequently, what my great-grandfather emphasised was not so much fine play, as fair play. That is to say, that playing skillfully is only one small part of the process. Playing fair, respecting the laws, is the more significant part, he used to say. I am told that he had devoted himself to educating the students in this spirit, in this philosophy. Thus, throughout the 100-plus year history of Japanese rugby, the enjoyment of playing rugby was subordinated to the spirit of fair play. In this way, I am so proud of my great-grandfather Ginnosuke Tanaka.'

From Keio, the game – a reflection of Japanese society's intricate rules and customs – spread to Japanese universities and then percolated into the high-school system where, based on Ginnosuke Tanaka's formula of 'play hard, play fair', it became the main winter team sport. In 1910 a rugby club was founded at Third High School, while in 1911 Doshisha University got the ball rolling and Keio University took on the team of the Third High School. The first inter-university match, between Keio and Doshisha, was played in 1912, the same year when rugby started at Kobe University and at the Kyoto Prefecture First Junior High School. The Japanese Union was formed in 1926 and the first overseas tour was to Canada in 1930, with the Canadians returning the

visit in 1932. The first Japan Football championship, sponsored by Osaka Mainichi Newspapers, was launched in 1918, while the Hanazono Stadium in Osaka, the first rugby stadium in Asia, built by Osaka Electric Orbit Co. and home to the Japanese Schools tournament, was opened by Prince Chichibu, brother of Emperor Hirohito, in 1929. The war temporarily halted the progress of rugby, but in the early 1950s rugby football, no doubt helped by the old martial-arts traditions resurrected in the rituals and customs of the game, recommenced its triumphant match through schools and universities. By 1980 there were more than 70,000 registered players and 3,000 teams.

Japanese rugby has undergone major changes during the last four decades. The century-long traditions of the Japanese game based on high school and university rugby lasted until the 1980s, when company (corporation) rugby took over. The last 20-odd years, as the game embarked on its most traumatic journey – the transition from amateurism to professional sport – were probably the most significant, with the recruitment of foreign players for the domestic league a natural extension of the new professional game. The launch of a professional franchise, Sunwolves, in Tokyo, as part of the Super Rugby Series, has contributed to the evolution of a playing elite, which made the extraordinary success against South Africa in 2015 RWC possible. The icing on the cake was without doubt the decision of World Rugby to grant the JRFU the right to organise the 2019 RWC, which in the long term should elevate rugby to the top of the pyramid in Japanese sport. One hopes that the edifice built with such care by generations of players and administrators will survive the decision to end the Sunwolves franchise after 2020. Will World Rugby step in?

TOP Keita Inagaki of the Sunwolves during the franchise's first Super Rugby match, *v.* Lions, 27 February 2016; Lions won 13–26.

RIGHT Cute kids but a serious point: Japan now has more registered players of all ages than Ireland, Wales or Scotland.

In today's environment, the hunter's *all-active* approach is more important than ever.

At times like these, the financial world can be both complex and daunting. And yet, there are still healthy Profits to be had. For those active enough (and astute enough) to track them down. The truth is, for the seasoned hunter, today's environment is just another action-packed instalment in their continuing story.

ARTEMIS
The PROFIT Hunter

2

RUGBY WORLD
CUP 2019

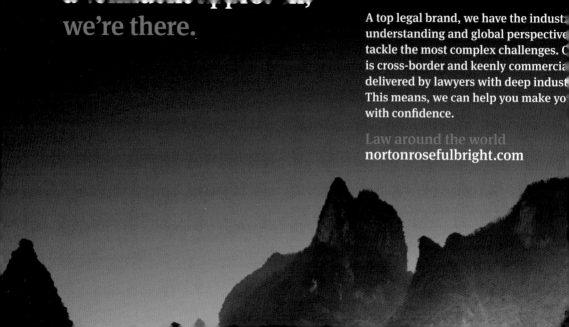

Pool A: Japan in Charge
BRAVE BLOSSOMS TRIUMPH

by **PETER O'REILLY**

That evening, we saw play Japan play heavenly rugby to seize top spot and to claim their rightful place at rugby's top table, in the knock-outs for the first time.

A little embarrassingly, one of my favourite memories of the 2019 Rugby World Cup is of watching a game in a bar in Fukuoka. Imagine. Your employers spend a fortune to send you half-way around the world. The office manager spends hours sending emails back and forth to get you accredited for games. And the rugby correspondent ends up watching the action in a boozer?

An explanation is required. The game in question was Japan v. Scotland, the day after Typhoon Hagibis had swept through Yokohama. All transport was down. We were confined to Fukuoka, where Ireland had played Samoa the previous day.

I'm envious of those reporters and fans who witnessed Japan's victory live. The atmosphere in the stadium, by all accounts, was special. But so, too, was the atmosphere in 'Two Dogs', a medium-sized hostelry in

Ireland wing Jacob Stockdale leaves Scottish tacklers in his wake during his team's emphatic opening win.

Kenki Fukuoka, a second-half replacement, races through to score Japan's try against Ireland.

downtown Fukuoka, populated that evening mainly by locals, with a small smattering of Irish fans. It was a raucous, emotional, uplifting evening, and the perfect climax to what was the most fascinating, complicated, controversial and surprising of the four World Cup pools: Pool A.

Why the perfect climax? Because that evening, we saw play Japan play heavenly rugby to seize top spot and to claim their rightful place at rugby's top table, in the knock-outs for the first time, and to claim their place in the nation's hearts.

Some, like Scotland coach Gregor Townsend, grumbled that the Brave Blossoms had been given too many advantages. Not only were they allowed to play the final pool game, thus knowing their exact requirements for qualification, but they also played the first. Whereas a team like Scotland had to make do with one four-day turnaround, the tournament schedulers spread Japan's games as evenly as possible to afford them the maximum recovery time between matches.

It was clear that Rugby World Cup Inc. wanted Japan to qualify. It made sense from a commercial point of view but also from the point of view of growing the game in a newish, large and potentially lucrative market. They hardly wanted a repeat of 2015, when the hosts left the party prematurely.

If there were a few whines initially, they were drowned out by the acclamation for Japan's brilliant rugby. The spirit of their defence and especially the brilliance of their attack made them everyone's second-favourite team – or favourite team in the case of those wonderfully engaged and enthusiastic local fans.

That Japan embraced this tournament was made official by the TV viewing figures for the game against Scotland. Those figures peaked at 53.7 per cent of the population, averaging at 39.2 per cent – meaning that over 60 million people were watching at the height of the excitement towards the end of the game. In other words, the TV audience had more than doubled since the opening game of the tournament, against Russia.

I was actually at that game, incidentally. Nothing in Japan's performance suggested that they would ultimately top the pool. It had been another clever idea to pit them against the lowest seed in the tournament first up, to give them a push-start, so to speak. And they needed that boost. Understandably, they looked nervous, perhaps burdened by the expectation of victory. An early error by full-back Will Tupou allowed Russian wing Kirill Golosnitskiy the honour of scoring the first try of the tournament.

Japan won 30–10. It was probably no harm for the occasion that Russia gave a decent account of themselves for their pre-tournament form had been wretched, with defeats by Jersey, from the English Championship, and by Connacht, in Russia. The Rugby World Cup gods wanted Japan to win but they didn't want a massacre. They also wanted some box-office gold and they got it in the shape of Kotaro Matsushima, the wing, who scored a hat-trick of tries and ran with dash and zip. The increase in volume inside the stadium whenever Matsushima ran into space would become a theme of the tournament.

Importantly for Japan, Matsushima's third try, in the 70th minute, also secured a valuable bonus point. 'Just getting the bonus-point win today was huge,' Luke Thompson told me in the mixed zone after the game. 'We weren't pretty today. There was a lot of pressure on the boys. It was essential if we're going to achieve our goal of making the knock-outs. Now we can just concentrate on playing Ireland.'

Thompson had an interesting story to tell. The 38-year-old Kiwi qualified to play for Japan by residency and had recently come out to retirement because the lure of playing in a fourth world cup, and on 'home' soil, had been irresistible. Japan had been ordinary that evening but I got a flavour of their determination to cause a shock when I asked him if he expected Ireland to target the Japanese scrum when the teams met on the second weekend of the tournament. 'Well, they can try,' Thompson said, chest out. 'They're more than welcome to. We back our scrum. We scrummed against South Africa a couple of weeks ago and we had no problems at all.'

First, Ireland had to play Scotland in Yokohama, the game that just about everyone outside of Japan saw as being the defining game of the pool – the two so-called Tier One teams battling it out supposedly to decide who would top the pool, in somewhat alien conditions – wet and windy but also warm. There was bad blood between the sides, we heard – perhaps the familiarity of the PRO14 breeding contempt. We expected a war. But Scotland never turned up.

After Ireland's surprisingly one-sided 27–3 victory, all accusations of flakiness aimed at the Scots seemed justified. Townsend had chosen as many leaders as possible, and his side had a record number of caps for a Scottish selection. The Irish pack simply blasted them aside, and it showed on the scoreboard: three first-half tries, all scored by members of the Irish front five, all from short range. Ireland were just too good in contact, and the Scots never got to put pressure on Jordan Larmour, Ireland's inexperienced full-back, who actually helped to set up the bonus-point try for Andrew Conway in the second half.

To make matters worse for Scotland, they lost flanker Hamish Watson to a knee injury. 'It was disappointing,' Townsend said afterwards. 'We didn't start with the energy, accuracy or aggression required to beat a team like Ireland.' And how come? Townsend was unable to answer that one.

So Ireland had won what everyone saw as their toughest game. I made the mistake – along with many others, I should add – of presuming that the next three weeks would be just a matter of marking time before a quarter-final date with South Africa. It looked all too predictable. But this pool was anything but predictable.

Flanker T. J. Ioane of Samoa is tackled by Grant Gilchrist (4) and Magnus Bradbury of Scotland. Much improved Scottish tackling was the foundation of their 34–0 bonus-point win, which included two penalty tries.

Twenty minutes into the Japan *v.* Ireland game in sultry Shizuoka the following Saturday, everything was going according to form. Ireland had scored two tries and led 12–3, despite the absence of Johnny Sexton, who'd aggravated a groin muscle in the Scotland game and was replaced by Jack Carty, who was making only his third Test start. Carty was going nicely, and so were Ireland. If there was a turning point, it might have been a line-out over-throw by Ireland captain Rory Best, which gave Japan turn-over ball, which is when they can look their most lethal. Japan didn't score directly from that mistake but they did get into some rhythm, and they did look to be getting stronger as half-time approached, whereas Ireland seemed to be wilting slightly in the humidity.

This wasn't an illusion, either. Watching long periods of unbroken play during the second half, you realised the massive advantage Japan enjoyed in terms of conditioning. They were super-fit and also super-skilful on the ball, with the scoring pass from centre Timothy Lafaele to Kenki Fukuoka a prime example. That score put Japan in front for the first time with 22 minutes remaining – plenty of time for a comeback, you thought. In the end, Ireland needed some heroic defence from Keith Earls to cling on to a bonus for losing by seven points.

Japan 19 Ireland 12 – a sensational result and a sensational performance. Who was waiting for us in the mixed zone but our old friend, Luke Thompson. 'Everyone had written us off,' he said. 'All the Irish media were talking about South Africa and how they are going to play them in the quarter-finals and what they had to do. So we know what we have to do. It's a very special moment.'

Sexton, meanwhile, tried to inject a positive spin the following day, suggesting that defeat could be a blessing in disguise. 'In the last two world cups that I've been involved in, we've not cruised through the group but we've had everything go our way in the pool stages,' Sexton said. 'And then we've had the day that we had yesterday in a quarter-final … and we'd be going home today. The great thing now is that we've got the rest of the pool to get things together.'

But Ireland were less than impressive beating Russia 35–0 in horrendously humid conditions indoors in Kobe. Then they watched as Japan bagged another bonus-point win over Samoa, that bonus coming in controversial circumstances well into injury time. Coming into the final week, Ireland reckoned they still had their destiny in their hands, knowing that a bonus-point victory over Samoa in their final game would ensure them a quarter-final.

The one thing they couldn't control was the weather, however. Early in the final week of the pool,

Japanese winger Kotaro Matsushima is all smiles after scoring the controversial last seconds bonus-point try, following the surprising decision to penalise Samoa for a crooked scrum feed.

ABOVE Scrum-half Dwayne Polataivao of Samoa tackles Yury Kushnarev of Russia during Samoa's 34–9 win.

RIGHT George Horne of Scotland scores his third and his team's seventh try during their 61–0 victory over Russia.

Super-Typhoon Hagibis was tracking towards Fukuoka. Everyone went scrambling for the tournament rules and found, to their horror, that if a game had to be cancelled for any reason, each side would be awarded two points. It was unthinkable.

Ultimately, Ireland's game against Samoa was unaffected by the weather. Ireland won 45–7, with Sexton imperious. That was their quarter-final booked, even if the identity of their opponents was uncertain. New Zealand or South Africa? It all depended on the weather.

Hagibis had veered east, causing games in other pools to be cancelled, and tragically causing loss of life as well as enormous damage to property and infrastructure. Suddenly, a couple of cancelled rugby matches didn't seem such an important matter. Still, for the integrity of the tournament, World Rugby desperately needed that final pool game – Japan *v.* Scotland – to go ahead.

Remarkably given Hagibis's ferocity, which caused landslides in places like Kamaishi, the pitch at Yokohama Stadium was declared fit that Sunday morning. Scotland went into the game confident, having notched a couple of big wins since the Ireland defeat – 34–0 against Samoa, 61–0 against Russia. They duly scored first, with Finn Russell dancing past a couple of defenders. The way Japan responded gave the tournament some of its most memorable moments.

Even a thousand kilometres away in Fukuoka, watching on a big screen in 'Two Dogs', you could sense the emotion in the stadium, with pictures of grown men weeping during a haunting rendition of the Japanese national anthem before kick-off. A brief silence was held to honour those who had died the previous day.

Soon, the emotions were all joyous, as Japan went on the rampage. Kenki Fukuoka produced an outrageous off-load to send Matsushima away for the first try. A flurry of off-loads set up a brilliant try for loose-head prop Keita Inagaki. Everyone, from 1 to 15, can run and handle and cause havoc. Or kick. Ryoto Nakamura's delicious grubber set up the third try, by Fukuoka.

When Fukuoka scored a fourth just after half-time to nail yet another bonus, Japan were delirious. To their credit, Scotland rallied. They did so convincingly to put doubts in some Japanese minds, at least where we were watching. This made victory only sweeter. On the final whistle, delirium.

Later, Thompson provided some perspective. 'There was a lot of talk about the game not going on and there are people losing their lives and their homes,' he said. 'We are just playing a sport and if we can offer some hope or motivation – just a little break from the loss and sadness that some people are experiencing – that's a huge thing for us.

'Unlike four years ago, we're no longer sneaking in under the radar and we have beaten two Tier-One teams and finished top of our pool. We have created history and some pretty amazing things for Japan rugby, but the tournament is not finished.'

OPPOSITE, TOP Man of the match Kenki Fukuoka scores his first and Japan's third try just before half-time in the dramatic final pool match.

OPPOSITE, BELOW Scotland prop Willem Nel's 50th minute try threatened to spark a second-half fight-back.

BELOW Japan's players celebrate their well-deserved success at the final whistle.

Pool B: All Blacks Ahead
ADVANTAGE NEW ZEALAND

by **NEALE HARVEY**

After their opening-match confrontation, New Zealand and South Africa moved serenely into the knock-out stages, with the challenges set to become harder.

Japan's opening night victory over Russia naturally enough dominated newspaper and TV headlines but we did not have long to wait for the first clash of the giants as defending champions New Zealand strode into Yokohama for their highly anticipated showdown with South Africa. The Springboks, confidence boosted after winning the Rugby Championship, which included a highly creditable 16-all draw against the All Blacks in Wellington, had been transformed over the previous 12 months under head coach Rassie Erasmus and fancied their chances of making an early statement of intent, having seen the odds on them winning a third World Cup tumble sharply.

By contrast, New Zealand's warm-up form had been patchy after a defeat to Australia, a bitty, error-strewn win in Argentina and that draw against the Boks, and the pattern looked set to continue as South Africa, with heavyweight forwards Eben Etzebeth and Malcolm Marx bullying their way over the gain-line and half-backs Faf

RIGHT Scott Barrett en route to scoring the All Blacks' second try against South Africa in the crucial pool opening match.

BELOW RIGHT Older brother Beauden Barrett, playing unusually at full-back, clashes with South Africa's wing Cheslin Kolbe.

BELOW Pieter-Steph du Toit scores his side's first try as the Springboks begin their second-half fight-back.

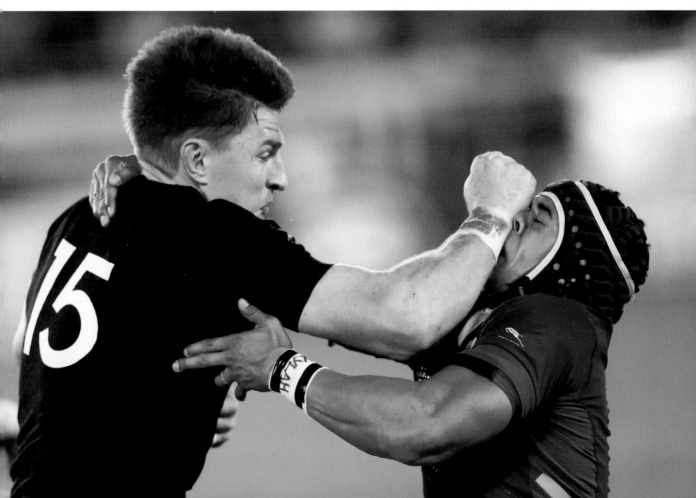

Jake Polledri of Italy bursts through Namibian tackles during their opening pool match. Polledri scored a try in the 47–22 victory after coming on as a replacement early in the second half.

de Klerk and Handré Pollard putting the All Black back three under huge pressure with a stream of high kicks, came out firing in the opening 20 minutes.

It was just the kind of heavyweight contest the World Cup needed but, to their credit, Steve Hansen's Kiwis refused to buckle and when Pollard missed a penalty to double an early 3–0 lead and a loose pass from De Klerk enabled New Zealand to gain crucial momentum, the holders showed their class to rack up 17 points in five sensational minutes – all the products of Springbok errors.

De Klerk's initial poor pass allowed Richie Mo'unga to hack downfield, after which the fly-half notched a penalty to tie the scores. Then, when fluffed aerial challenges by South Africa handed New Zealand further easy possession, the All Blacks required no second invitation to rip the Springboks apart with superb handling and support play for tries by George Bridge and Scott Barrett.

'Most of their scores came from turn-overs or bad kicks,' lamented Erasmus afterwards. But at least he could take heart from a rousing second-half revival that saw Pieter-Steph du Toit's try and a further five points from the boot of Pollard reduce New Zealand's lead to four before the Kiwis steadied the ship with penalties from Mo'unga and Beauden Barrett to run out 23–13 winners – a convincing night's work that reaffirmed their status as tournament favourites.

'Were we perfect? No, but you're never going to be at this stage,' mused New Zealand supremo Hansen. 'You arrive not in the swing of things and you've got the biggest game of the group. Everybody knew this was going to be a big match and both teams played very well at times.' With injured talisman Brodie Retallick set for a return, the All Blacks were on the march.

Italy's best chance of making a dent in the big two's ambitions was to win their opening matches against rank outsiders Namibia and Canada and then throw everything into game three against South Africa. Conor O'Shea's men came in on a desperate run of 11 defeats in 12 games, their only succour being provided by an 85–15 World Cup warm-up victory over Russia in August, but they achieved their initial objectives by beating Namibia 47–22 and an underpowered Canada 48–7.

Canada's decline since the heady days of the 1990s when, with men like Al Charron and Norm Hadley in their pomp, they defeated Wales and France and pushed the likes of New Zealand, England, Australia and

South Africa close, is a rugby tragedy. At this World Cup, they proved no match for the Italians before being hammered 63–0 by New Zealand and 66–7 by South Africa before their final match against Namibia was washed out by Typhoon Hagibis – a dismal end for them.

Back to the Italians, though. Could they upset South Africa, who in the meantime had disposed of Namibia 57–3 to get their challenge under way after that opening-day disappointment? The answer would be 'no' in a match that will chiefly be remembered for the continuing brilliance of Springbok wing Cheslin Kolbe and the sending off of Italian prop Andrea Lovotti for dumping Bok number 8 Duane Vermeulen on his head just after half-time as Italy pressed South Africa's line.

'Crass stupidity,' raged O'Shea, whose side had trailed 17–3 at the break but had been showing encouraging signs of getting back into the contest. In fact, the Italians were lucky not to have two men dismissed simultaneously with Nicola Quaglio equally culpable in an incident that drew comparison with the assault by Tana Umaga and Keven Mealamu on Brian O'Driscoll during the British & Irish Lions tour of New Zealand in 2005. You could only wonder what was going through their minds.

From that moment onwards it was one-way traffic for South Africa as Kolbe added his second try to a sizzling first half effort, before Lukhanyo Am, Makazole Mapimpi, R. G. Snyman and Marx helped themselves to further scores as the Boks rounded off a 49–3 win to put the Italians, who in recent years appear to have gone backwards at a startling rate of knots, firmly in their place.

Meanwhile, Namibia's part-time collection of farmers, dentists and bank clerks, under the direction of former Wales lock Phil Davies, had put up a decent fight against the Italians before running into a fired-up South Africa. Their resolve had not been weakened, however, by the time they faced up to New Zealand, despite many pundits predicting the Kiwis would post 100 points plus.

Not a bit of it. After 35 minutes the All Blacks were just 10–9 ahead, testament to the Namibians' fast defensive line and a determination to contest fully at the breakdown. Hooker Torsten van Jaarsveld led the way for Namibia, for whom Damian Stevens notched three penalties to counter New Zealand tries from Sevu Reece and Anton Lienert-Brown, before a semblance of order was restored in the lead-up to half-time when All Blacks

Number 8 Braam Steyn of Italy goes over for the first try during the Group B game with Canada in Fukuoka; Italy won comfortably with seven tries in a final score of 48–7.

prop Angus Ta'avao and full-back Ben Smith both crossed.

Seven second-half tries ensured the final score-line blew out to 71–9 but the efforts of the lion-hearted Namibians had won them many friends. 'The scoreboard's not very pretty at the end but the effort and the commitment … I'm so proud of the players with how we tried to play and certain things that we actually did, which is pleasing,' said Davies, whose side will now return to rugby's backwaters as pleas for improved funding and more meaningful competition continue to be made.

With South Africa's thrashing of Canada assuring them of a quarter-final place, only two matters remained to be resolved, with New Zealand needing a win over Italy to clinch top spot and Namibia and Canada battling just for pride and the avoidance of the wooden spoon. Sadly, neither match took place – Typhoon Hagibis took care of that – with Namibia denied their chance of a first-ever World Cup win and Italian legends Sergio Parisse and Leonardo Ghiraldini missing their swansongs.

The loss of life in Japan put rugby into perspective, but it still seemed an unsatisfactory way to conclude a pool that had only briefly flickered to life before New Zealand – awarded two points for the postponed fixture – and South Africa moved serenely into the knock-out stages, where they would meet Ireland and Japan respectively, with the challenges set to become harder. Would New Zealand's round-four cancellation leave them under-cooked for their impending quarter-final?

Looking ahead to his side's clash with the Irish, ranked the world's top team going into the tournament, Hansen opined: 'They are a quality side, they've been number one this year, and [our] last three results [against Ireland] are loss, win, loss so there won't be any complacency in our camp. It's pretty exciting. We are right where we want to be.'

With memories of South Africa's defeat by Japan in 2015 still fresh, Erasmus insisted: 'Brighton is in the past. Both teams have improved since then and it will be interesting to see how each of us handles the pressure of expectation. You can feel the vibe. They are excited about it and they should be because their team is doing very well. We know we are in for a very tough game.'

By the time this is in print, we'll know if New Zealand retained their crown or whether South Africa downed hosts Japan before fulfilling their undoubted potential.

Pool C: Weather Intervenes
BUT ENGLAND TOP THE POOL

by **SARA ORCHARD**

Three comfortable bonus-point wins for England set up the decider that northern hemisphere fans wanted to see, but the 'Typhoon Gods' finally had different ideas.

England, France and Argentina loomed over Pool C. The three rugby giants were all expected to make the quarter-finals by their unions and fans. Ultimately one would be left disappointed, whilst Tonga and USA would make sure that any passage for the big three was far from smooth.

The opening Pool C match was an absolute corker. Nearly 50,000 fans packed into the Tokyo Stadium to watch the showdown between France and Argentina. The rugby world waited to see if the French could finally break away from the usual clichés. It turned out to be one of the best matches of the pool stages; however, all French rugby clichés you can think of applied.

As three-time finalists, France have never failed to make the Rugby World Cup knock-outs, so it is safe to say they like the big stage and the opening 40 minutes allowed coach Jacques Brunel's men to shine. Tries from centre Gaël Fickou and scrum-half Antoine Dupont, along with two penalties, gave Les Bleus a commanding 20–3 half-time lead. The notion of 'champagne rugby' was bandied around and the resurgence of France as a

RIGHT Joe Cokanasiga (L) and Jonathan Joseph of England chase back under pressure from Cam Dolan of the USA.

BELOW RIGHT Joe Cokanasiga scores his second try in England's 45–7 win over the USA.

BELOW Prop Rabah Slimani of France looks set to take on most of the Argentina pack during the pool's opening match.

global superpower became regular reading on social media.

But then came the second half. Mario Ledesma's Argentina didn't reach the 2015 semi-finals through fluke. Los Pumas have a team that can draw on big-game experience, especially after the success of the Jaguares in reaching the Super Rugby final in 2019. The come-back was launched with tries from Guido Petti and Julián Montoya, while replacement fly-half Ben Urdapilletta would slot two penalties to give Argentina the lead.

France hadn't scored a point in the entire second half until Brunel deployed replacement fly-half Camille Lopez to make the difference. Making his first-ever appearance at a World Cup at the age of 30 and with 11 minutes left on the clock he slotted a drop goal to give France the 23–21 win. It left the European side in charge of the pool and Argentina with something the size of Mount Fuji to climb to make the quarter-finals.

The next day the Sapporo Dome hosted England and Tonga. Since England won the Rugby World Cup in 2003 their performances at the tournament have gone downhill, culminating in them being knocked out of their own World Cup at the group stage in 2015. Led by coach Eddie Jones, however, this time they were expected to make light work of the Pacific Island nation.

Despite the hype surrounding England, Toutai Kefu's Tonga brought their physicality in spades. Captain Siale Piutau was making his third appearance at a World Cup and his side's sheer muscle held the English onslaught for 20 minutes until centre Manu Tuilagi scored twice in quick succession allowing the favourites to head in at half-time 18–3 ahead.

England hookers Jamie George and his replacement Luke Cowan-Dickie scored tries in the second half, while captain Owen Farrell would end the match kicking 15 points. With just one Sonatane Takulua penalty to Tonga's name the match would finish 35–3 to England. They now topped the table with the bonus-point victory, a position they wouldn't relinquish throughout the pool stage.

The USA would join the party in Kobe as England had a four-day turnaround to prepare to face the Eagles. The USA had only won three World Cup games before 2019 but had shocked many by qualifying ahead of Canada to take the top spot for the Americas.

Led by South African Gary Gold, USA were keen to show that their new professional league at home, Major League Rugby, was bearing fruit. However, this match was very one-sided. England would go on to score seven tries and in the second half USA were reduced to 14 men on 69 minutes when open-side flanker John Quill was red carded for a late and dangerous tackle on England's Owen Farrell. The incident ended Quill's World Cup, as he became one of seven players who would be shown red cards in the pool stage. England continued to dominate the pool on maximum points following the 45–7 win.

By the second weekend of the competition Argentina had licked their wounds and were ready to take on Tonga at the Hanazono Rugby Stadium in Osaka. They needed a big win and they delivered a stunning performance in the first half. A hat-trick for hooker Julián Montoya was completed in a 19-minute spell. He became the first hooker to complete the hat-trick feat at the World Cup since 1999.

This was all in the first 40 minutes and Los Pumas went in at the break with a try bonus-point confirmed and 28–7 up on the scoreboard. Tonga would score a second try through Telusa Veainu after the break but the damage had been done. The Sea Eagles were winless and pointless in the table while Argentina would go second until France played again midweek.

The USA were keen to make amends after their tough opener with England but their next outing was against another European powerhouse opponent. France against the USA was played at the Fukuoka Hakatanomori Stadium in Fukuoka City. The French powered out the blocks with wing Yoann Huget scoring within five minutes, but although Alivereti Raka would chalk up a second try the French only went in 12–6 up at the interval. The boot of USA fly-half A. J. MacGinty was keeping the Eagles in touching distance and another penalty in the second half saw the USA stay within three points of the French until 66 minutes. All of a sudden French indiscipline was forgotten and three more tries secured the 33–9 win. It left France second in the table and the USA rooted to the bottom.

Argentina knew they had to beat England if they were to have any chance of making the quarter-finals. The clash between the two heavyweights would take place back in Tokyo in the same stadium where Los Pumas had lost to France in their opener. Mario Ledesma surprised with his team selection as former captain Augustín Creevy, playing at his third World Cup, was dropped to the bench. The other notable change was the omission of fly-half Nicolás Sanchez; Argentina's all-time leading points scorer didn't make the match-day 23.

England were keen to show their strength as two notable names appeared on their bench. Prop Mako Vunipola and wing Jack Nowell were primed to make their first appearances at the tournament after both being out injured for long periods.

As the media once again licked their lips at another heavyweight clash, a red card in the first half would taint the game. Argentina lock Tomás Lavanini was sent off on 17 minutes for a high tackle that made contact with the head of England captain Owen Farrell. With only 14 players, the task of holding back England proved too much for Argentina. Six tries for England meant they had three bonus-point wins, topped the group and were the first team at the 2019 Rugby World Cup to qualify for the quarter-finals. Argentina's chances of progressing rested on the hopes that France would trip up.

For their third match the French would put out a side to face Tonga that had eleven changes from the one that had beaten the USA. Coach Jacques Brunel tested his third different half-back combination of the tournament as Baptiste Serin wore 9 and Romain Ntamack 10.

Fans at the Kumamoto Stadium watched France dominate and by half-time they led 17–7. It left many to wonder if Tonga's World Cup would ever get going. Luckily that didn't last long. The second-half saw the Sea Eagles score a second converted try within six minutes to take the score to 17–14. Two penalties made Les Bleus more comfortable until the 78th minute when flanker Zane Kapeli scored for Tonga. The conversion by Latiume Fosita took the score to 23–21. Memories from the 2011 World Cup when Tonga had beaten the French 19–14 in Wellington flooded rugby minds, but the clock wasn't kind and France held on to scrape into the quarter-finals with a game to spare.

Finishing third in the pool would secure Argentina's place at the next World Cup in 2023. If they could win their final match with the USA it would also save some of their blushes, since this would be their first World Cup since 2003 when they wouldn't qualify from their pool.

Centre Gaël Fickou makes a break against the USA as France accumulate the 33–9 bonus-point win they want.

The Kumagaya Rugby Stadium in Saitama Prefecture hosted this highly entertaining feast of rugby. Ten tries would delight the watching fans. Argentina provided seven of them and finished 47–17 winners. Los Pumas ended their World Cup journey knowing they would be attending the next World Cup. As for the USA they still had one last match to try and record a win.

As anticipation grew for the clash between England and France to determine the pool winner, a storm in

Tonga hooker Paula Ngauamo runs past USA number 8 Cam Dolan during the final Pool C match, won 31–19 by Tonga.

the Pacific began to grow. Typhoon Hagibis will forever leave its mark on RWC2019 and on the Pool C final standings. The match due to be held in Yokohama on the final weekend was cancelled. Within the rules of the competition the game was deemed a 0–0 draw and two points were awarded to each side. Neither side complained about the missing fixture, with England head coach Eddie Jones going as far as to say the 'Typhoon Gods' were smiling down on his side. England topped the pool with France finishing second.

However, Pool C was not over and its conclusion became USA versus Tonga and a race to avoid finishing last. It was Tongan captain Siale Piutau's birthday and before the match he'd announced that this game would be his last wearing the red shirt. The same was true for flanker Sione Kalamafoni. Both men were appearing in their 12th Rugby World Cup game, breaking the Tongan record in the process. With other notable internationals like Italy captain Sergio Parisse denied their swansong due to the typhoon, Piutau and Kalamafoni would be allowed to wallow in theirs.

The Hanazono Stadium in Osaka witnessed the last Tongan *sipi tau* led by Piutau as the battle of the Eagles against the Sea Eagles began. Tonga were favourites and took an early lead as prop Siegfried Fisi'ihoi scored the opening try. However, despite Tonga enjoying more territory and possession in the first half it was the USA who went in 12–7 up at the break. USA captain Blaine Scully, playing at his third World Cup, had to be substituted early in the match with injury and it was his replacement who powered the Americans onto the scoreboard, Mike Teo'o scoring two tries in just five minutes.

Finally the Tongans began to show their class. Three more tries eventually saw them secure their first win of the 2019 Rugby World Cup. The last try scored by Telusa Veianu came on 80 minutes to seal a bonus point and give the final say of the match to the Tongan captain. Piutau had already been named player of the match before his last act on the international rugby pitch was to knock over the conversion. Final score 31–19 to Tonga.

It meant Tonga finished fourth in the pool and USA last. However, the feeling was one of celebration after an enthralling conclusion to Pool C with the USA coach Gary Gold saying in his post-match interview: 'Just look at the amazing supporters and the people in the streets. The whole event has been amazing.'

Pool D: Wales Challenged
URUGUAY SURPRISE FIJI

by CHRIS HEWETT

The victory over Australia was proof positive that in the mind-set department, Wales were as strong as any side in the tournament. And strong they had to be.

Blame Reece Hodge, the spindly Australian who set the ball rolling and watched it gather pace for the rest of the pool stage, rolling ever faster downhill until it smashed through the door of the World Cup disciplinary office and sent the men in business suits flying in all directions. From the moment the Melbourne Rebels wing made shoulder-to-head contact with the significantly more substantial and infinitely more powerful Fijian back-rower Peceli Yato after 24 minutes of the opening Pool D contest in Sapporo, the tournament had trouble written all over it.

Strange to relate, nothing much happened in the immediate aftermath of the Wallaby's patently illegal no-arms challenge close to the corner flag. Nothing, that is, except for the early demise of Yato, who left the field for a concussion check and promptly failed it – a result that also denied him a place in the Pacific Islanders' side for the following game with Uruguay. Yes, that would be the same Uruguay who proceeded to turn the group on its head by beating the Fijians against all expectations, including, if truth be told, their own. Under the circumstances, Fiji could have done with Yato that day. After all, he had been their best player against the Australians, scoring a try and rampaging around like a world-beater before being 'Hodged'.

Quite how the match officials reached their joint conclusion that the hit on Yato should go un-punished remains a mystery – not to mention something of a scandal, given the fact that Hodge went on to score a try of his own in a 39–21 victory. Perhaps it was because Yato, very much sinned against, was stampeding his way towards the Wallaby line with such breathtaking

Peceli Yato of Fiji makes a break during the early stages of the Australia v. Fiji game, before his clash with Reece Hodge.

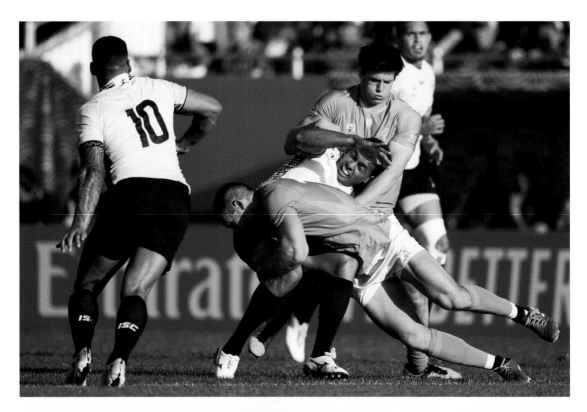

Georgia number 8 Otar Giorgadze scores under the posts in his team's match with an understandably weary Uruguay in Kumagaya on 29 September.

momentum that Hodge, patently the sinner, seemed equally hard done by as he was sent flying through the air with the greatest of ease by the impact. But the replays of the incident exposed the truth of the matter and the ensuing rumpus went on for days, setting a dark tone for the rest of the competition.

Michael Cheika, the Wallaby coach, arrived in Japan with many strands to his reputation. A lifelong interest in Trappism was not among them. After Hodge's inevitable citing, but before the disciplinary hearing in Tokyo, he accused the Fijians of failing to act 'in the spirit of the game' by raising the incident with the authorities. To which John McKee, his opposite number, responded, with some restraint: 'Maybe Michael Cheika's views of what's within the spirit of the game are slightly different to those of some other people, but it's not up to me to decide what exactly he meant by that comment. From our side, we lost a player who was nearly the most influential on the park … And because of the head injury he can't play against Uruguay either, so we've already lost out.' For the record, Hodge was banned for three matches.

That was not the half of it. With head-high contact now the major talking point, players from all corners of the union landscape found themselves on the wrong end of yellow and red cards. What was more, the referees caught it in the ear almost as badly as Yato and his fellow victims, if only in the figurative sense. World Rugby, the sport's supreme governing body, publicly accused the officials of failing to meet standards. Ouch. 'Elite match officials are required to make decisions in complex, high-pressure situations and there have been initial challenges in the use of technology and team communication, which have impacted decision-making,' their statement continued. Double ouch. Cheika himself would have struggled to make his point more forcefully without descending into the vernacular.

ABOVE LEFT Ben Volavola of Fiji is tackled by Uruguay's Tomás Inciarte during Uruguay's remarkable 30–27 win.

LEFT Uruguay full-back Felipe Etcheverry and prop Facundo Gattas (both replacements) celebrate at the final whistle.

Still, the Wallabies were at least sitting on a bonus-point victory after cutting loose in the second half – a couple of quickfire subterranean tries from the spherical hooker Tolu Latu broke the Fijian resistance, followed by some slightly more athletic scores from the likes of Samu Kerevi and Marika Koroibete – and with Wales matching them blow for blow by running Georgia ragged in the opening quarter, the stage was set for the long-anticipated meeting of the two 'contenders' at the Tokyo Stadium. But first, there was a shock to the system in the shape of that Fiji–Uruguay match.

The South Americans did not have so much as a cat's hope. That much was obvious. They had not faced a top Test nation since the 2015 World Cup – not even Argentina, which according to most atlases remains within walking distance of Uruguay – and while a small handful of their number were playing rugby in England or France, none of them were performing at the top level. Yet somehow, they won. It was one of the great displays of rugby heroism, a triumph of attitude over adversity, of unsparing commitment over sporting common sense, of enthusiasm over pretty much everything else. Yes, the Fijians were damaged by events against the Wallabies. Yes, some of their prime performers – the wing Vereniki Goneva, the captain Dominiko Waqaniburotu – were miles off their level. Yes, their goal-kicking was just about as bad as could possibly be imagined. But the contributions of such home-based, low-profile, semi-professional-at-best individuals as the wing Nicolás Freitas and the hooker Germán Kessler, along with the reliable line-out deliverer Manuel Leindekar and the resourceful half-backs Santiago Arata and Felipe Berchesi, were nothing short of astonishing. The fact that the small town of Kamaishi, so horribly ravaged by the 2011 tsunami, should have played host to this sporting miracle seemed entirely appropriate.

Thanks to the brutalities of Rugby World Cup fixture scheduling, not as unashamedly stacked against the smaller nations as was once the case but difficult to deal with all the same, Uruguay were back in action four days later, a short while before the Australia–Wales collision that would decide the final standings. Georgia were their opponents this time and the after-effects of the Fiji game were clear to anyone with a functioning pair of eyes. The heat in Kumagaya was every bit as extreme as the tiredness in the limbs of the South Americans, who wilted under the heat applied by the iron loose-head prop Guram Gogichashvili (a 21-year-old scrum specialist with a big future, hence his place on the payroll of top-end French club Racing 92) and struggled to cope with the full-frontal carrying of the number 8 Otar Giorgadze. Five tries and a 33–7 victory were the rewards for the Eastern Europeans. Uruguay? They lost Facundo Gattas, their replacement prop, to a red card. His crime? A head shot. What else?

That same day in Tokyo, the big hitters traded punches. All the early work came from Wales, who rediscovered the lost art of the early drop goal, as opposed to the last-roll-of-the-dice variety, and succeeded in shaping the first half of the game to their own design. Dan Biggar's three-pointer, a try from the centre Hadleigh Parkes and a trademark interception strike from the scrum-half confidence trickster Gareth Davies were the foundation stones of a 23–8 interval lead and as they were blessed with a defensive strategy lovingly pieced together by Shaun Edwards, there seemed no way back for the Wallabies. But the green-and-gold types are well versed in the ways of World Cup performance and even though Rhys Patchell, on at number 10 for the stricken Biggar, copied his elder and better with a drop goal to extend the advantage, Wales slowly ran out of possession, territory and just about everything else that counts as currency in a game of rugby. Strong off the bench, the Australians notched tries from Dane Haylett-Petty and the ever-industrious flanker Michael Hooper and had they opted for an attacking line-out rather than a shot at the sticks while the Welsh were suffering from tackle fatigue, they might have completed their comeback. But they didn't. Matt To'omua duly landed his penalty shot, but the only subsequent score was a similar effort from Patchell, impressively cool in managing what was left of the contest. Under their coach Warren Gatland, the Welsh had developed a habit of losing close games to Australia. If you're going to break bad rugby habits, World Cups are as good a place as anywhere and far better than most.

Gatland had not enjoyed an easy time of it since arriving in Japan. Short of lock forwards after Cory Hill's failure to recover from long-term injury and Adam Beard's outbreak of appendicitis on the way to the airport, he also found himself numerically challenged on the coaching front when Rob Howley, an important member of his think-tank for more than a decade, was summoned home to face allegations of a breach in betting regulations. A weak-minded group would have struggled to cope with the upheaval, yet Gatland trusted his senior players – the centre Jonathan Davies and the indefatigable Biggar, the hooker Ken Owens and the magnificent captain Alun Wyn Jones – to hold the party together. The victory over Australia was proof positive that in the mindset department, Wales were as strong as any side in the tournament.

And strong they had to be. Victories by Fiji and the Wallabies over Georgia and Uruguay respectively meant that if Wales wanted to top the pool and give themselves a marginally softer route through the knock-out phase – the likelihood was always that the Pool D winners would have France and South Africa in their half of the

draw, rather than England and the All Blacks – they could not afford to mess up in their remaining fixtures. More to the point, they were fully aware that Fiji equalled danger. The history said as much: Gatland was appointed Wales coach in 2007 largely because the Fijians had dumped Wales out of that year's World Cup at the group stage. Add to this the fact that Fiji's performance against Georgia in their third outing had been something close to outstanding, with brilliant displays from Levani Botia, Frank Lomani and the off-the-scale wing Semi Radradra, and there was good reason to worry.

In some respects, the Wales–Fiji meeting in Oita was as thrilling as anything yet seen in the competition. With Radradra wreaking havoc across the field and his fellow wing, Josua Tuisova, getting into the swing of it after a rough spell of form, the all-court attacking threat posed by the islanders was above and beyond. Witness the corner-flag finish from Tuisova, who rode tackles for fun in opening the scoring – a finish of such jaw-dropping strength that barely half a dozen wings in World Cup history could have dreamed of matching it. Jonah Lomu? Rupeni Caucaunibuca? They had it in them, for sure. And the rest? Answers on a postcard, please.

Wales had to think their way through the challenge and if it took them a while, they got there in the end. Josh Adams was the headline responder, the Worcester wing bagging three tries of contrasting styles – the first

from an aerial kick, the second from a straight spin off phase play and the third from a Davies off-load. Only the middle score could be classed as a run-in. But there was more to it than Adams, notably the capacity of the back-rowers Josh Navidi and Ross Moriarty to meet the Fijians on the gain-line and win crucial inches. For those watching, it was a lot of fun. For those playing, it must have hurt like hell.

Even then, the pain was not over. Not for Wales, not for the Wallabies. Those ultra-plucky Uruguayans might have won the first half against Australia but for a couple of tight refereeing calls, while the Georgians refused to go away when the two-time champions tried to hit them hard from the get-go in the final round of games. With a Gorgodze here (Mamuka), a Gorgadze there (Beka) and a pair of centres everywhere (Davit Kacharava and Merab Sharikadze), the Lelos' tackle count was in three figures by the half-hour mark – a ridiculous statistic, by any measure – and it was not until the formidable Koroibete completed a broken-field score off a generous bounce that the outcome could be considered beyond doubt.

As for the Welsh, they suffered similarly against Uruguay. The usual suspects – Freitas, Berchesi, Kessler – made life a misery for their much-changed opponents and there was precious little return for the favourites until a rush of points at the last knockings. Where next for Wales? The last eight.

Where next for Uruguay? Complete invisibility for four years. Thanks for coming, gents; you've been stars. See you in 2023.

ABOVE Josh Adams just makes the line as Fiji full-back Kini Murimurivalu arrives just too late.

BELOW Young replacement prop Rhys Carré of Wales makes a break during Wales's final pool match, with Uruguay.

Quarter-Final 1
ENGLAND RAISE THEIR GAME

by **CHRIS FOY**

The England team responded well. They coped with expectation. They flew back to Tokyo with the main weight of pressure removed – ready to shoot for the stars.

The facts and figures were impressive enough. When England beat Australia in their World Cup quarter-final in Oita, it was a seventh consecutive win over the Wallabies; they amassed 40 points and earned a first semi-final appearance for 12 years.

These were all momentous feats, but there was even more to it than that. This was a result which had especially profound implications, both in the short term and further down the line.

Going into the latest encounter between familiar 'Ashes' foes, there had been speculation that England might be under-cooked, due to the cancellation of their last pool game, against France, because of the arrival of Typhoon Hagibis. They insisted they could alleviate the issue with the intensity of their training. Hindsight suggests they were right.

Australia certainly hit the ground running and put pressure on the scrambling English defence early on. But once Eddie Jones's side established a foothold, they

Australia lock Rory Arnold is just too late with his tackle on England centre Henry Slade.

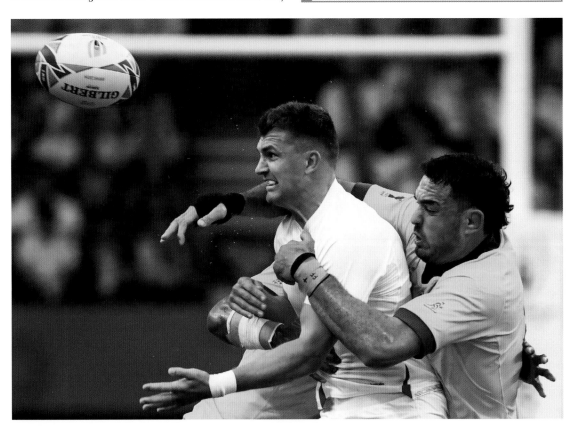

gradually assumed control, in keeping with their status as the clear favourites.

There were various decisive factors behind what became an emphatic dismissal of dangerous rivals. The first was that Jonny May marked his 50th Test appearance by demonstrating the predatory instincts which are his trademark. The Leicester wing was presented with two scoring chances in quick succession and he took both of them. Suddenly, midway through the first half, the Wallabies found themselves playing catch-up.

When Michael Cheika's men set about that daunting task, they ran into another problem. Well, two, to be precise: Tom Curry and Sam

Underhill. This was the occasion when the English apprentices eclipsed the Australian masters. The young Red Rose flankers embellished soaring reputations by utterly up-staging the iconic pair collectively known as 'Pooper' – David Pocock and Michael Hooper.

Curry was named Man of the Match, for a performance of staggering dynamism and influence. He won turn-overs, he was an imposing mainstay of the defensive effort and he even showed the composure and handling skill to set up May's first try. As for Underhill, his sledgehammer tackling routine ensured that many an Australian raid faltered behind the gainline.

Another England player who produced a personal tour de force was Kyle Sinckler. Here was further proof of how the Harlequins prop has developed and matured. Some early scrummaging problems saw the tight-head targeted by the Wallabies. Not so long ago, the wind-ups would have had the desired response, but not this time. Instead, with soothing support from team-mates close by, he kept his head and had his revenge.

There were two stand-out moments for Sinckler in the second half. First came his maiden Test try, as he ran a perfect line to take Owen Farrell's flat pass and burst clear to score. He celebrated with arms out-stretched and a huge grin on his face; providing the defining image of the match. Up in the stand, his mother watched on and Jones later spoke of how she was 'proud as punch'.

Sinckler's other key contribution was to steal possession and allow England to end a prolonged siege in their 22. The break-out and the celebrations that followed signalled that Australian resistance had been decisively overcome.

Jones had one of those days when all the decisions he had made were vindicated. There had been major doubts cast on the wisdom of demoting George Ford to the bench, in order for Farrell to reclaim the number 10 shirt. But the captain responded with an imperious display, to move on from his stuttering efforts in the previous outing against Argentina.

Mako Vunipola was thrust back into England's first-choice XV for his first start – for club or country – since early May. If he was rusty, it didn't show. The Lions loosehead ran and carried and tackled himself into the ground. When he was replaced, he sat on the bench, shattered, with ice on his neck, tissue jammed into his nostrils and blood on his shirt. It was another of the day's striking images.

In the aftermath of the game, the obvious source of most English pleasure was the way they had responded to the fight-back by Australia. From a commanding position, Jones's side found their lead cut to one point, at 17–16. But this time – unlike in the recent past – they didn't panic. This time, they regathered and surged clear again.

That surge came as a relief to Jones. He knew all about the profound implications in Oita. He knew that he and his team were operating on a knife-edge. There had been enough talk about win or bust – do or die. That is the essence of knock-out sport, but that wasn't the full story.

England lock Courtney Lawes rises high with the help of his supporters to win tidy line-out ball.

After taking over in the aftermath of a World Cup failure, Jones was well aware that a quarter-final defeat would be regarded as another one. Despite presiding over an era of success since replacing Stuart Lancaster, the Australian was in no doubt about the stark equation. If England had lost, he would have been removed from his post. For his RFU employers, reaching the last four was a minimum requirement, so this result ensured at least a pass mark.

It removed the necessity for the union's new chief executive, Bill Sweeney, to oust a coach whom he had worked with before – one he respects and admires. The RFU had committed vast resources to Jones's World Cup mission and if his team had been stunned by his compatriots, there is very little chance he would have survived.

Instead, it was his old club-mate Cheika who paid the price of defeat and failure. After a long spell of trouble, this was the final straw. He had always hinted at leaving his post after the tournament and, sure enough, he stood down the day after the loss to England – with a parting shot aimed at his union and its chief executive. He had become a divisive figure and his departure was inevitable. Four years earlier, Cheika's impressive salvage operation had led the Wallabies all the way to the World Cup Final at Twickenham, but the 2019 showpiece was an almighty come-down for them. They dropped to seventh in the global rankings, behind the rising sons of Japan.

At least the Australians were given some cause for hope about better times ahead. While Curry and Underhill represented the new wave of England players emerging as pedigree Test stars, there was a glimpse of an exciting new Wallaby talent. Cheika had thrust teen sensation Jordan Petaia into his back line at outside centre and the tyro was by no means over-awed by the grand occasion. Amid the rubble of a wrecked campaign, Australia had a consolation to cling on to.

But the day belonged to England, it was just a shame that the stadium wasn't full to witness their impressive exploits. Officially, there were 8,000 English fans in attendance and they out-numbered the Australian spectators

Smiles from England's Anthony Watson, and Tom Curry in the background, as Watson runs in the final England try.

two-to-one, but there were thousands of empty seats in the Oita Dome.

Local infrastructure could not cope with such large-scale events – back-to-back quarter-finals in the space of a single weekend. There was a chronic shortage of hotel rooms, along with access issues at the venue, which led to long delays for supporters after the game.

However, for the England team, it had been a galvanising experience. They dispelled the fears that they might be under-cooked. They coped with expectation. They responded well when their opponents fought back. They reached their minimum-requirement target and ensured there would not be the sort of brutal post-mortem which followed the last two World Cups.

It was a liberating process. They flew back to Tokyo with the main weight of pressure removed – ready to shoot for the stars.

ENGLAND 40		AUSTRALIA 16	
1 Mako Vunipola	13 Henry Slade	1 Scott Sio	13 Jordan Petaia
2 Jamie George	14 Anthony Watson	2 Silatolu Latu	14 Reece Hodge
3 Kyle Sinckler	15 Elliot Daly	3 Allan Alaalatoa	15 Kurtley Beale
4 Maro Itoje		4 Izack Rodda	
5 Courtney Lawes	*Replacements*	5 Rory Arnold	*Replacements*
6 Tom Curry	16 Luke Cowan-Dickie	6 David Pocock	16 Jordan Uelese
7 Sam Underhill	17 Joe Marler	7 Michael Hooper (c)	17 James Slipper
8 Billy Vunipola	18 Dan Cole	8 Isi Naisarani	18 Taniela Tupou
	19 George Kruis		19 Adam Coleman
9 Ben Youngs	20 Lewis Ludlam	9 Will Genia	20 Lukhan Salakaia-Loto
10 Owen Farrell (c)	21 Willi Heinz	10 Christian Lealiifano	21 Nic White
11 Jonny May	22 George Ford	11 Marika Koroibete	22 Matt To'omua
12 Manu Tuilagi	23 Jonathan Joseph	12 Samu Kerevi	23 James O'Connor

Quarter-Final 2
ALL BLACKS DOMINANT

by **RUAIDHRI O'CONNOR**

'We could have played really well and they could still have gone over the top of us ... You have to be nailed on against them and we weren't nailed on.'

On a balmy Saturday night in Tokyo, the team who came into the World Cup as the world's No. 1 side came face to face with the side universally recognised as the best in the business. It was billed as a battle between two coaching heavyweights, with the loser facing into his final match. The fifth and last clash between them since 2013, with the score standing at 2–2.

If Joe Schmidt did one thing during his time in charge of Ireland, and he did many, it was to earn the respect of his native New Zealand. Perhaps he did that job too well. Steve Hansen's side arrived at this quarter-final and delivered their best performance in four years, blowing Ireland away in the process. They'd had a long wait for this game due to their meeting with Italy being cancelled as a result of Typhoon Hagibis and they proved too fresh, too fast and too skilful for an Irish side who barely laid a glove on the World Champions.

In the 11 months since losing to the same opposition in Dublin, the All Blacks revolutionised their

New Zealand's flanker Ardie Savea at the heart of another powerful All Black drive. Sam Whitelock (5) and Kieran Read (8) are among the supporting players on hand.

style of play and displayed real ruthlessness in picking their team. Rieko Ioane, Ben Smith and Ryan Crotty watched from the stands as a backline featuring Beauden Barrett, George Bridge, Anton Lienert-Brown, Jack Goodhue, Sevu Reece, Richie Mo'unga and Aaron Smith tore Ireland apart on the back of a clean, quick

supply of ball provided by a forward-pack that dominated the Irish eight.

It was ruthless, relentless and a joy to watch unless you happen to be Irish.

For the team of 2018, it was a humbling experience and a disappointing way for Schmidt and his captain Rory Best to bow out. Both men lingered long on the Tokyo Stadium pitch to say their goodbyes, as Kieran Read and Co. made their bows to the crowd and moved on to the semi-finals.

'We shot ourselves in the foot and New Zealand capitalised on it. It's hard enough playing against them with our A game, never mind our D game,' winger Keith Earls said, summing things up from an Irish perspective. They were poor, but New Zealand were sensational and they punished the Irish errors without hesitation.

Before the game, the atmosphere was electric as the huge travelling Irish contingent in the crowd sang 'The Fields of Athenry' as the All Blacks performed the *haka* and the team took a collective step forward as they had done before their win over the same opponents in November last year. Unfortunately for them, they were on the back foot for the rest of the night.

New Zealand silenced the green army quickly, racing into a 10–0 lead within the first 14 minutes, with Mo'unga kicking a penalty and Aaron Smith darting over from close range after a series of dominant carries from the New Zealand forwards.

'We prepared for this game with a lot of intent – very thorough, and the prep was awesome,' Mo'unga said. 'We went into this game with no stone unturned, and [this] gave us the best chance to put a good performance out.

'It's a quarter-final of the World Cup. You don't need any extra motivation. We know the importance of the game, and we know that this week's a bit different. But that's why we were able to get up and bring so much intent in that game.'

They didn't ease off the pace, punishing Johnny Sexton's missed touch and a line-out mix-up by delivering superbly off a scrum on half-way. Jack Goodhue's quick hands released Sevu Reece and, when Keith Earls stopped him short, Smith exploited Jacob Stockdale's error for his second.

'I get a bit of stick for not running more. I'm always a person who runs when it's on. I was looking a lot this week at footage with chances around the breakdown. For a run, there were opportunities and I'm just really happy I took them,' the All Black scrum-half said of his brace.

Facing an uphill battle, Ireland tried to pull out one of their moves but when Rob Kearney and Sexton got in a muddle, the out-half lost the ball thanks to a thundering Reece tackle and Mo'unga hacked on for speedster Barrett to control superbly and score.

With the All Blacks up 17–0 after 31 minutes, the game was essentially over and whatever Schmidt said at half-time went out the window when Stockdale got his co-ordinates wrong and stepped into touch, handing New Zealand another chance to strike. They duly delivered, with the brilliant Kieran Read finding Codie Taylor on his shoulder. By then, it was a matter of how much and if Ireland could muster something.

First, Matt Todd scored his side's fifth try before Robbie Henshaw got Ireland off the mark. George Bridge finished the try of the night, then Todd stopped C. J. Stander illegally at the post, conceding a penalty try and shipping a yellow card. Jordie Barrett finished the scoring with New Zealand's seventh to finish at 46–14.

At the end, the camera lingered on a haunted Schmidt whose time coaching Ireland had ended with a record World Cup defeat. 'We would love to have got into the top four. That is the one thing that continues to remain elusive. Heartbroken would not be far away from how I feel and how the players feel,' he said.

'After the November series we wanted to make sure this was our target and maybe it consumed us too much and we got distracted from the focus. You have to make them work for everything. In the past we had forced them to do that even when we lost against them. Then we were chasing the game and if you are chasing the game against the All Blacks you are going to give them opportunities and that is exactly what we did.

'We could have played really well and they could still have gone over the top of us. They are stifling, made it hard for us to breathe. When we did have opportunities to breathe we gave them oxygen back. You have to be nailed on against them and we weren't nailed on.'

Schmidt's opposite number Hansen paid tribute to the Ireland coach, but was keen to focus on how well his own team had played, particularly in defence. 'It's massive, isn't it?' he said.'Defence is 50 per cent of the game and probably 90 per cent when you take in the psychological value of it. We kept our discipline, and when they carried, we made punishing tackles that forced some errors and then teams start to second-guess a little bit and psychologically you get an edge. We'll enjoy our moment, it was a special Test match, one that the All Blacks, New Zealanders and the players can be proud of.'

RIGHT As so often, forward power laid the platform. Kieran Read carries, supported by the formidable Brodie Retallick.

BELOW Irish tight-head Tadhg Furlong by contrast cannot escape the All Black grasp.

They marched on to meet England; Ireland were going home and for their vastly experienced captain the end had arrived in the worst possible way. 'I'm tired, sore, upset,' Best said. 'You focus on what has just gone. We have a lot of characters in that dressing room [and it's] not often you get one that is deadly silent. There are big men in tears and that is what happens when you put heart and soul into something.

Rory Best of Ireland leaves the pitch following what is to be his final international. On an emotional occasion, he was warmly applauded by the All Blacks and their fans, as well as the thousands of Irish supporters and neutrals at the game.

'That was an incredibly tough Test match. They are incredibly focused. We have been looking at this and all our focus has been on the World Cup that we forgot to win the little battles along the way.'

Their wait for a first semi-final goes on for another four years, but New Zealand had no such hang-ups.

NEW ZEALAND 46		IRELAND 14	
1 Joe Moody	13 Jack Goodhue	1 Cian Healy	13 Garry Ringrose
2 Codie Taylor	14 Sevu Reece	2 Rory Best (c)	14 Keith Earls
3 Nepo Laulala	15 Beauden Barrett	3 Tadhg Furlong	15 Rob Kearney
4 Brodie Retallick		4 Iain Henderson	
5 Sam Whitelock	*Replacements*	5 James Ryan	*Replacements*
6 Ardie Savea	16 Dane Coles	6 Peter O'Mahony	16 Niall Scannell
7 Sam Cane	17 Ofa Tuungafasi	7 Josh van der Flier	17 Dave Kilcoyne
8 Kieran Read (c)	18 Angus Ta'avao	8 C. J. Stander	18 Andrew Porter
	19 Scott Barrett		19 Tadhg Beirne
9 Aaron Smith	20 Matt Todd	9 Conor Murray	20 Rhys Ruddock
10 Richie Mo'unga	21 T. J. Perenara	10 Johnny Sexton	21 Luke McGrath
11 George Bridge	22 Sonny Bill Williams	11 Jacob Stockdale	22 Joey Carbery
12 Anton Lienert-Brown	23 Jordie Barrett	12 Robbie Henshaw	23 Jordan Larmour

Quarter-Final 3
WALES SCRAPE THROUGH

by DAVID STEWART

A few seconds are all it needs to separate the joy and release of victory from the despair of a likely triumph thrown away in a 'moment of madness'.

It has been eight years. Sam Warburton. Alain Rolland. Welshmen, not all of them wearing red-tinted glasses, feel that with a more sympathetic refereeing interpretation in the 2011 semi-final, the team coached by Warren Gatland – then as now – would have made the final, and been able to spoil New Zealand's party in a way the French could not quite manage (whether you include Craig Joubert in the indictment, or not).

Gatland was supposedly able to list a full-strength side in Oita, despite significant injury in the pool stages to the likes of Dan Biggar and Jonathan Davies; few were surprised when Davies withdrew before kick-off, replaced by Owen Watkin. The French, with the exception of those already invalided home, were – for a change – able to get their best troops on the pitch at the same time. The 'turf accountants' made Wales favourites, with a six-point start.

Then came Sébastien Vahaamahina. The 28-year-old, originally from New Caledonia, could live to be 100 years old, become Secretary-General of the UN, cure cancer, solve the world's climate issues, and still the first

Sébastien Vahaamahina (wearing dark scrum-cap) scores France's first try after five minutes.

Flanker Charles Ollivon breaks away to score his try and give France a handy 12-point lead with only nine minutes gone.

paragraph of his obituary will recite the moment of madness when his right elbow was driven into the side of Aaron Wainwright's head, leading to a red card and a mortal blow to his country's prospects of a fourth World Cup final. The French will have to wait four more years, and home soil again, before another attempt to secure their first Webb Ellis Cup.

It was such a shame. In the overworn cliché of recent years, the French team that neutrals wanted to see actually did turn up. Their sparkling running and handling from deep, unusually tied into a structure the players seemed to understand and adhere to (the influence of Fabien Galthié perhaps), dominated the first 47 minutes of one of the the best games of the tournament.

The Clermont lock opened his team's account after only five minutes, when as the astute Andrew Mehrtens observed: 'If there is one thing the French know how to do, it's pick 'n drive.' Romain Ntamack's conversion struck the post; little did we know what influence said woodwork would subsequently have: 5–0.

A mere couple of minutes later, France extended their lead with a gorgeous try from their own half. Possession from a right-sided line-out was swept across the midfield, for the extravagantly talented Virimi Vakatawa (one of many Fijians now playing in the French leagues) to break the line before the ball was transferred inside via the supporting Antoine Dupont, resulting in wing-forward Charles Ollivon crossing. The added points meant the French had an early 12-point lead, and the mood music had us wondering whether they might run away with the game, literally and metaphorically.

No, Aaron Wainwright, has developed – in his short international career thus far – a reputation for being at the places where things happen. Still only 12 minutes had elapsed when the clearly inspired Guilhem Guirado – who, in recent years, sometimes held his team together single-handedly – drove the ball up at the back of a line-out just on half-way, only to lose it in contact. The young Dragons back rower took advantage of the error to run in from 40 metres, Biggar converting: 7–12. With a quarter of the match gone, the out-half added a penalty, and Wales were back to a two-point defecit while – on the run of play – hardly being in the contest.

Unlike the Saturday matches, and the later Japan against South Africa contest, physios and other personnel in luminous bibs were not forever disturbing play. When they now did so, for the first time, it had been so hectic that a breather seemed welcome – as much in the stands as on the pitch. A glance at the coaches' box revealed a remarkably composed Jacques Brunel, a visibly relieved Gatland. At this point, Wales won a line-out. It seemed symbolic that the delivery was so untidy, Gareth Davies had to bob 'n weave merely to make serviceable possession from it.

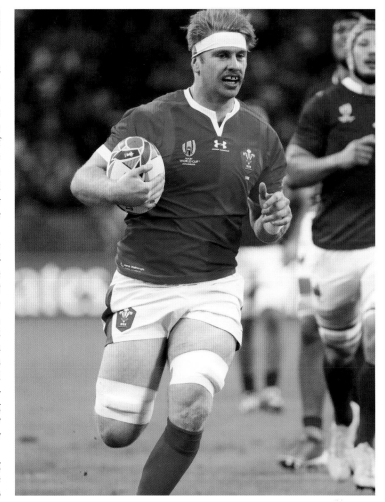

Aaron Wainwright races for the line to score Wales's first points

On 27 minutes, Josh Navidi left the field with a hamstring injury. The resigned expression as he departed the arena suggested the Cardiff skipper had started with the problem. Ross Moriarty (nephew of Richard, captain of Wales in the original 1987 tournament) came on. Immediately Ntamack delivered a beautiful right to left cross-kick for Gaël Fickou, who was taken high by the Welsh replacement: yellow card.

This meant France were opposed by only 14 men until half-time. Immediately, Vakatawa was the beneficiary of a clever number 2 jumper/hooker handling exchange at the front of a French line-out, followed by a delightful off-load from Damian Penaud. The try was a splendid example of Les Tricolores managing to combine individual brilliance with team organisation – gaps being created, runners taking them. That said, Wales clearly missed Jonathan Davies, their key defensive organiser

France looked like scoring again, but a series of phases in the Welsh 22, which should have led to a scoring pass on the right wing, was so clumsy that Penaud was left trying to imitate Eric Cantona instead of strolling over from a textbook delivery. Then, on 36 minutes, Ntamack hit the post with a penalty, an error which would prove crucial.

In that final spell before half-time, there was a sense that French brilliance and domination needed to be reflected in additional points. Wales were fortunate not to receive a second yellow card for persistent offside; Mr Peyper was being lenient.

Resuming at 19–10, Camille Lopez replaced Ntamack. Something of a drop-goal specialist, he should have done better with a chance from fairly adjacent to the posts only three minutes into the second half. Liam Williams then got bolshie again when disputing the decision of a touch judge, seemingly unaware the ball had been touched in flight.

Verbals are one thing, physical violence another, as would be seen when France looked all set to score from the ensuing line-out. That man Vahaamahina again secured the catch and drive, before scrum-half Dupont went blind seeking to put an outside runner across in the corner. That thrust was held, but then a television replay revealed the horrible elbow use. It would be fair to say the action was in retaliation for some neck interference by Wainwright, but it was of an instinctive and vicious kind which has been all too common within French rugby over the decades.

None were in any doubt this might be a vital turning point, and that those opportunities not taken by the French either side of half-time could prove ever so costly. Still, that they held Wales to three points over the next 25 minutes was a tribute to Gallic spirit and organisation, but a few seconds are all it needs to separate the joy and release of victory from the despair of a likely triumph thrown away in a 'moment of madness'.

It is no consolation to French followers that the winning try was somewhat dubious. With only six minutes left, their seven-man scrum finally cracked, the ball squirting loose in a peculiar manner into Welsh possession

Moments that turned the contest.

ABOVE Welsh celebrations begin after Ross Moriarty scores their decisive late try.

ABOVE LEFT Romain Ntamack, who played beautifully in the first half, evades Justin Tipuric (7) and George North, but his two kicks that hit the post proved costly.

LEFT Sébastien Vaahamahina's moment of madness as Aaron Wainwright feels the power of his elbow.

once replacement scrum-half Tomos Williams had tackled Ollivon. Had it gone forward from a Welsh hand? There was doubt, consultation between the TMO and the South African referee, but the score was confirmed.

Needless to say, Biggar, who had narrowed the gap with a penalty on 53 minutes, nailed the match-winning conversion – no woodwork issues for him: 20–19. Gatland was gracious in defeat: 'the better team lost'. However, the scales of justice in rugby, as in life, have a curious way of levelling out over time – Warburton, for one, is entitled to feel that way.

WALES 20		FRANCE 19	
1 Wyn Jones	13 Owen Watkin	1 Jefferson Poirot	13 Virimi Vakatawa
2 Ken Owens	14 George North	2 Guilhem Guirado (c)	14 Damian Penaud
3 Tomas Francis	15 Liam Williams	3 Rabah Slimani	15 Maxime Médard
4 Jake Ball		4 Bernard Le Roux	
5 Alun Wyn Jones (c)	*Replacements*	5 Sébastien Vahaamahina	*Replacements*
6 Aaron Wainwright	16 Elliot Dee	6 Wenceslas Lauret	16 Camille Chat
7 Justin Tipuric	17 Rhys Carré	7 Charles Ollivon	17 Cyril Baille
8 Josh Navidi	18 Dillon Lewis	8 Gregory Alldritt	18 Emerick Setiano
	19 Adam Beard		19 Paul Gabrillagues
9 Gareth Davies	20 Ross Moriarty	9 Antoine Dupont	20 Louis Picamoles
10 Dan Biggar	21 Tomos Williams	10 Romain Ntamack	21 Baptiste Serin
11 Josh Adams	22 Rhys Patchell	11 Yoann Huget	22 Camille Lopez
12 Hadleigh Parkes	23 Leigh Halfpenny	12 Gaël Fickou	23 Vincent Rattez

Quarter-Final 4
END OF JAPAN'S DREAM

by ALAN LORIMER

Japan's group stage successes had fired the imagination of fans throughout the rugby world. Could they surpass expectations and make it to the semi-final?

The big question going into the last of the quarter-finals at the Tokyo Stadium was: could Japan go one further than their already massive achievement of reaching the last eight? To do so, Japan needed to invoke the spirit of four years earlier when the Brave Blossoms produced the shock result of the 2015 tournament with a 34–32 defeat of South Africa in the English seaside town of Brighton.

In the following four years, Japan had built on their Brighton breakthrough under head coach Jamie Joseph – the successor to Eddie Jones – and assistants Tony Brown and Scott Hansen by preparing assiduously for the 2019 Cup. Confirmation that Japan had got their preparation right came in bucketloads during the pool stage as the Brave Blossoms set about rearranging the world order with wins over Ireland – top-ranked going into the competition – and then, by an identical seven-point margin, Scotland.

Four years had also changed South African rugby. In the relatively short time since stepping into the top job, new coach Rassie Erasmus had hauled the Springboks out of a temporary slump, before guiding his side to victory in the southern hemisphere's 2019 Rugby Championship.

Other than their hard and losing match against New Zealand in the opening game, South Africa were never stretched in their other pool games, the huge scores against Namibia, Canada and Italy offering evidence of the ease with which they secured qualification for the

South Africa winger Makazole Mapimpi scores his team's first try, taking advantage of weak Japanese tackling earlier in the move.

knock-out stage. These one sided-matches also ensured that South Africa had near maximum energy level for the quarter-final.

Japan's group stage successes (four from four) and their style of play had fired the imagination of the host nation, and of fans throughout the rugby world. But would the high-tempo game that had produced victories over Tier One countries Ireland and Scotland cut the mustard against South Africa? Could Japan surpass expectations and make it to the semi-final?

Several analysts suggested that Japan had fulfilled their ambitions by reaching the quarters. It was also contended that Japan's victories in the pool stage had been achieved with an over-reliance on their front-line players, and that their squad did not have the depth needed for a World Cup campaign.

Overlying this stage of the Rugby World Cup, of course, was the memory of Typhoon Hagibis, which a week earlier had devastated parts of the country and taken its toll on human life. Japan was consumed by the twin thoughts of typhonic destruction and the fairy-tale dream that their rugby team could truly mix it with the global elite.

South Africa had named a familiar starting side and a bench that comprised six forwards and two backs, shouting megaphonically their intended style of play. Japan head coach Jamie Joseph stuck to his trusted warriors, except at full-back where Ryohei Yamanaka replaced the injured William Taupou.

If South Africa oozed height, weight, muscularity and, it has to be said, pace in the back three, then Japan were all about players who flitted over the ground and who could handle the ball with exceptional accuracy. The match it seemed was a contest between a battleship and an ocean-going race yacht.

On 20 October 2019 it was an emotionally charged atmosphere in the 50,000-capacity Tokyo stadium that met the teams. Anthems over, it was then down to business. Japan looked enterprising from the kick-off but it was an unforced error that led to South Africa taking an early lead.

Pieter-Steph du Toit and Kotaro Matsushima contest a high ball. In this match Mutsushima had few of the running opportunities he had relished in earlier games in the tournament.

In an attempt to run the ball from Japan's 22-metre area fly-half Yu Tamura threw out a long pass to flying wing Kotaro Matsushima. The trajectory was conspicuously forward, resulting in an early scrum to South Africa some 17 metres in from the touchline.

The Springboks could not have asked for a better attacking opportunity but instead of releasing the ball quickly the powerful South Africa forwards put the squeeze on and shunted the Japan tight eight backwards. Scrum-half Faf de Klerk spotted that Tamura had been sent to guard the blind side and duly passed the ball to Makazole Mapimpi, who then flew past the tackling-

Lock Eben Etzebeth tackles Japan's tight-head prop Ji-won Koo, first capped for Japan in 2017.

averse Tamura before outpacing what defence could be mustered by Japan for an unconverted try in the corner: 5–0 to South Africa with just three minutes played.

If that score muted the huge home crowd then they soon rediscovered their voice some seven minutes later. But it was to shout their disapproval of a tip tackle by South Africa's formidable prop Tendai Mtawarira on his opposite number Keita Inagaki. The slow-motion replay showed the Japan front row's head and shoulder hitting the ground simultaneously, making the tackle a sending-off matter. Referee Wayne Barnes, after reviewing footage of the incident, eventually decided on a yellow card but was it only the Japan fans in the Tokyo Stadium who thought the punishment should have been greater?

Japan sublimated their sense of grievance into positive action by moving the ball wide with intricate passing that released pacy winger Kenki Fukuoka. The ball was then shipped infield and with momentum building it seemed Japan might pierce the Springbok defence.

Strangely, given the effectiveness of their backs, Japan used their forwards to finish off the attack on the opposition line only for their efforts to be met with solid resistance and ultimately a turn-over by centre Damian de Allende. A precious opportunity had been missed. Not quite though. At the next scrum, Japan's forwards extracted a penalty against the seven-man Springbok scrum allowing Tamura to atone for his earlier missed tackle with a three-point kick.

Seven minutes before half-time South Africa botched a scoring chance after Japan's talisman Michael Leitch had lost the ball in contact. The Springboks attacked on the blind side but when Lukhanyo Am was checked the centre's 'out-the-back' pass fell at the feet of Mapimpi, denying the winger a second try.

Then, in first-half stoppage time, South Africa yet again came close to increasing their points tally, this time De Allende powering through midfield before being tackled. The strong centre scrambled forward to touch down but referee Barnes immediately signalled in a way that would have won an award from the society of mime artists that the centre had crawled after being held in the tackle.

South Africa's slender 5–3 lead at half-time suggested a repeat of Brighton might be possible, but such hopes were quickly dampened by the Boks' power play and astute kicking from De Klerk that changed the dynamic of the game. From 5–3 at half-time South Africa moved into a 14–3 lead, following three penalty goals by fly-half Handré Pollard, the third of these after Japan's James Moore had been carded for a high tackle.

Then came the ultimate killer blow. As the game entered the last quarter, South Africa drove a line-out maul from just inside their own half until the moving mass rumbled to within 15 metres of the Japan line. When the maul then finally splintered, replacement hooker Malcolm Marx sprinted clear before putting De Klerk in for his side's second try, easily converted by Pollard.

Whatever one's views on the maul as a legal part of rugby, this was an immense show of power by the Springbok forwards, to which Japan, down to seven forwards at that point, had no answer. It finally killed off Japan's challenge and at the same time sent out a warning to others that South African's mauling game is a threat.

LEFT South African fly-half Handré Pollard looks set to secure possession despite multiple Japanese challengers.

BELOW Faf de Klerk finishes off the drive begun by South Africa's mauling power.

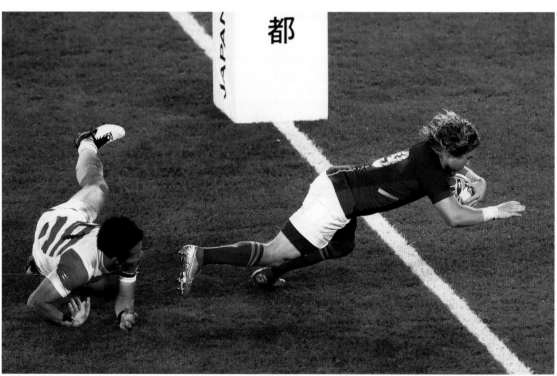

South Africa still had more misery to inflict on Japan. Replacement prop Isileli Nakajima was relieved of the ball by the twin efforts of skipper Siya Kolisi and replacement second row Franco Mostert. When the ball was moved wide Pollard sped through a gap before

Michael Leitch leaves the field to well-deserved, generous applause from Japanese and neutral fans.

linking with Willie le Roux whose finely judged pass sent Mapimpi racing to the line for his second try to give the Boks victory by 26–3.

It was a reminder that South Africa are back in business but it was also confirmation that Japan are capable of performing on the world stage. Moreover Japan's style of play reinvigorated the game of rugby and will surely have sold the sport to a new audience as viewing figures in the host country appeared to confirm. But if Japan's progress is to continue then the Brave Blossoms must be integrated into one of the two major annual tournaments. Over to you, World Rugby.

JAPAN 3		SOUTH AFRICA 26	
1 Keita Inagaki	13 Timothy Lafaele	1 Tendai Mtawarira	13 Lukhanyo Am
2 Shota Horie	14 Kotaro Matsushima	2 Mbongeni Mbonambi	14 Cheslin Kolbe
3 Ji-won Koo	15 Ryohei Yamanaka	3 Frans Malherbe	15 Willie le Roux
4 Luke Thompson		4 Eben Etzebeth	
5 James Moore	*Replacements*	5 Lood de Jager	*Replacements*
6 Michael Leitch (c)	16 Atsushi Sakate	6 Siya Kolisi (c)	16 Malcolm Marx
7 Lappies Labuschagné	17 Isileli Nakajima	7 Pieter-Steph du Toit	17 Steven Kitshoff
8 Kazuki Himeno	18 Asaeli Ai Valu	8 Duane Vermeulen	18 Vincent Koch
	19 Wimpie van der Walt		19 R. G. Snyman
9 Yutaka Nagare	20 Amanaki Mafi	9 Faf de Klerk	20 Franco Mostert
10 Yu Tamura	21 Fumiaki Tanaka	10 Handré Pollard	21 Francois Louw
11 Kenki Fukuoka	22 Rikiya Matsuda	11 Makazole Mapimpi	22 Herschel Jantjies
12 Ryoto Nakamura	23 Lomano Lemeki	12 Damian de Allende	23 Frans Steyn

The Quarter-Finals
WHAT THEY SAID

ENGLAND 40 AUSTRALIA 16

England coach Eddie Jones 'I was pleased the way players took it – stuck at the game. In the first 20 minutes Australia had 75–80 per cent of the play, moving the ball well. We had to defend really well and hung in there and got a bit of momentum back through our set pieces and then we took on a couple of good plays in the first half. They obviously got back in the second half through errors from us and we had to find our momentum and stick at it.'

On Owen Farrell 'Without trying to be too clever, that is how we thought the game would go. The first 30 or 40 they would run and we would be a lot on the defensive. Owen Farrell is our best defensive 10 for the first half. With George Ford coming on he was absolutely brilliant.'

England hooker Jamie George 'Staying level-headed when we are threatened is something we have been working on, especially after the draw against Scotland and the loss to Wales. In terms of mind-set when threatened we are a completely different team.'

England scrum-half Ben Youngs 'Everything that we rehearsed, practised and sat in meetings about when things got tight we were able to do. That was really pleasing to achieve in a huge game.'

Australia coach Michael Cheika 'I thought we played quite well for the first 50 or 60. We gave away two intercepts and they defended well. The better team won and you've got to suck that up sometimes. We were supposed to get things done for the people here and for Australians – I'm so disappointed.'

Australia captain Michael Hooper 'We played an attacking style of rugby which I think really threatened the English. What I think the English did really well was control the re-starts and we weren't able to exit our area well and on the flip side of that we weren't able to re-start and get back into the game the way we wanted. We are really upset. We emptied everything into this. We are pretty gutted for a lot of reasons.'

NEW ZEALAND 46 IRELAND 14

New Zealand coach Steve Hansen 'Numbers 1–5 lay the platform in my playbook. Numbers 6, 7 and 8 then get the benefits of those tight forwards doing their job and 9 and 10 get to drive the game and the way we're playing at the moment you have to chuck 15 in there as well.'

New Zealand prop Joe Moody 'We knew we had to give it to [Ireland] from the start and not let them build any momentum from that first kick-off. We kept the pressure on for the full 80 minutes. I think we can take some confidence out of it but at the same time it was still a tough game. I don't think the scoreline reflected how tough that game was.'

Ireland Coach Joe Schmidt 'We kind of gave them a leg up and when they get a points differential like that you are chasing the game. When you chase the game you take risks that if you are not executing perfectly they are going to capitalise on the back of it.'

Ireland captain Rory Best 'The onus was on us to win a quarter-final because then it becomes a habit. With Joe he helped take away some of the fear factor that the All Blacks held in the last three Tests. But when you do that they see you coming a lot more and when you get the best team in the world fully prepared and fully focused on you it becomes that little bit more difficult.'

Ireland lock James Ryan   'It felt like the speed of the game was very quick and they were attacking both sides of the ruck. When they're so good at that, it creates moving parts in our defence and it's more difficult to win collisions because they have so many different options. You start to soak a bit and when they have the threats they have, it makes it hard. On the other side of the ball, when you are making errors, it compounds that.'

WALES 20 FRANCE 19

Wales coach Warren Gatland   'The better team lost today and that red card was obviously significant. The thing about our boys is that they don't give up, they stick right to the end. It was a critical moment when we were down to 14 and they went for three points and hit the post. I think if they had gone to the corner and got some success it would have possibly been game over.'

Wales captain Alun Wyn Jones   'Our character showed through in the second half after the [red] card. We knew we had advantage at set-piece time and we wanted to take that advantage into their territory to give us opportunities, which we did. There is plenty for us to work on but I am pleased with the result.'

Wales back row Ross Moriarty   'It was very nerve-racking then to come back on and make sure there were no more mistakes or penalties. That is what I did and to put the ball down towards the end of the game was a very good feeling. It was probably the easiest try I've ever scored but probably the most nervous.'

France coach Jacques Brunel   'The outcome of the match is a very difficult thing to accept. The red card it is very clear. He had contact with his face so I don't have a problem with the decision. But I think the scrum at the end – we lost the ball. There is a player who pulled on the ball and it went forward and so that's the decision. I am a little disappointed.'

France lock Sébastien Vahaamahina   'I think I completely lost my head. I just lost control. I regret the act, admittedly it was spontaneous and out of control but the fact remains that I am responsible. I am the only one to blame.'

SOUTH AFRICA 26 JAPAN 3

South Africa coach Rassie Erasmus   'We are happy to make the semi-final. We were very nervous at half-time. We knew how they had played against Scotland and they were playing monumentally. At half-time leading by only a few points and leaving a few tries out there definitely the changing room was quiet. We had to come out of that lull and come and produce in the second half. The challenge at half-time was to get the guys' confidence up. I think that they did that.'

South Africa captain Siya Kolisi   'It was exactly what I expected. We knew what they were going to bring today and it took a lot out of us to keep on fighting. We fought and ground it out in front of this beautiful crowd. We knew how fast they can play the game, they play a style that is fearless and didn't shy away from it today. We pride ourselves in hard work in defence.'

Japan coach Jamie Joseph   'The last five minutes of the match epitomised this team. Having that willingness to never lie down is something I am incredibly proud of as their coach. That is the sort of thing that will help us going forward. I am going to celebrate the efforts and achievements of this team.'

Japan captain Michael Leitch   'Rugby is all about creating moments and taking opportunities. We had a few opportunities to capitalise on but unfortunately South Africa kicked us out. Congratulations to the South African team, they played their A-game and played it very well. I am not fulfilled or satisfied, just proud to be a member of this team. I told the players to keep their chins up. We don't have to look down. For the future we have to maintain this same attitude.'

Japan centre Ryoto Nakamura   'Our mentality has changed since Jamie Joseph became head coach.'

Semi-Final 1
ENGLAND POWER THROUGH

by **CHRIS HEWETT**

England showed a confidence under pressure that delighted Jones. It was a game where England came of age as a rugby force and the All Blacks were shown to be human after all.

This was arguably the greatest performance ever delivered by an England rugby team as they made the reigning Rugby World Cup champions look like also-rans in what was supposed to be a canter to the final. Instead of staying on course for a historic three-peat, Steve Hansen and his All Blacks trudged off to the third place play-off knowing their aura of invincibility at World Cups was consigned to the record books.

England set out their stall before the match even started by forming a V that took some of their players into the New Zealand half as they prepared to perform the *haka*. The match officials tried to get the England players back over the half-way line and although they would eventually be fined, it was a marker they wanted to put down and the All Blacks got the message.

It was an almost perfect 80 minutes from Eddie Jones's team, with a miscommunication between hooker Jamie George and the otherwise brilliant Player of the Match Maro Itoje the only blemish, which gifted a try to Ardie Savea to brighten his dark day. This was a match

ABOVE RIGHT England's dream start: Manu Tuilagi dives over from short range with barely a couple of minutes on the clock.

RIGHT Anton Lienert-Brown is crash-tackled by Maro Itoje, who immediately begins trying to strip the ball.

BELOW The *haka*, and England's innovative and successful response to the challenge.

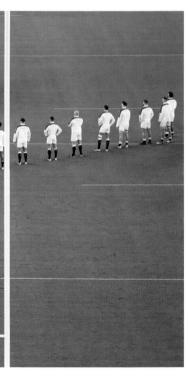

in which Jones won not only the bragging rights but also the tactical battle against the most successful international rugby coach of all time. As he reflected on the result, Hansen admitted that if he had his time again he may well have started with Sam Cane at flanker rather than Scott Barrett, who was drafted in at number 6 even though he is a second row.

Hansen and his fellow coaches believed that with England playing two open-sides in Tom Curry and Sam Underhill, they could severely pressurise the two recognised jumpers Itoje and Courtney Lawes. The plan back-fired spectacularly with Itoje and Lawes supported by the occasional leap by Curry, sticking to a line-out strategy devised by forwards coach Steve Borthwick that was almost perfect. With his line-out jumpers negated, Hansen had no alternative but to bring Cane on for the second half with New Zealand trailing 10–0.

The defending champions never found their momentum in the face of a suffocating England defence that had been worked so hard in training by coach John Mitchell; his charges performed so heroically that even

ABOVE Jonny May and Sevu Reece perform the aerial ballet as Elliot Daly and George Bridge are ready to support.

ABOVE RIGHT One that got away. Sam Underhill crosses for his 'try', soon to be disallowed.

RIGHT An all-too-rare sight from a New Zealand point of view: Brodie Retallick on the charge in the open field.

Ardie Savea goes over for New Zealand's try, with support from Dane Coles, but England stopped the All Blacks' come-back from going any further.

the All Black coaches were fulsome in their praise. The fact that one of their own – former All Black coach Mitchell – was at the heart of their pain must have made it even harder to stomach.

Hansen was magnanimous in defeat and said: 'You have to put your big boys' pants on and stand up and be counted. Congratulations to England. I think they were deserved winners tonight. You had two very good sides going at each other and the team that took the game won the game. We stepped up to the plate today and played as well as we could and we have to take it on the chin. Hard to stomach sometimes. See the character when we win and see it when we lose. We must stand up and be the same people we are when we lost.'

They not only lost, they were left beaten and bemused and the only attacks worthy of that description came late in the contest when another important tactical change was made to add Sonny Bill Williams to the midfield and his off-loads finally gave the dangerous Sevu Reece on the right wing chances to make ground. Beauden Barrett, playing full-back rather than number 10, also cut loose in the final quarter but was attacking from so deep that the brilliant England scramble defence snuffed out the danger.

In truth, this should have been a 30-point beating but England managed to have two 'tries' ruled out by the Television Match Official. First, the increasingly influential Underhill raced over only for a dummy-run by his partner in crime Curry to be ruled illegal because it stopped an All Black attempting a tackle. If that was clear-cut, the other incident was not. According to the TMO the ball went forward from one set of English hands to another in a moving maul before scrum-half Ben Youngs took over and darted through a tackle to reach the try line.

After the theatrical start thanks to the England V for Victory formation that had captain Owen Farrell and his smirk at its tip, what followed was a marvellous opening quarter, orchestrated with cool precision by George Ford who had been restored at 10 with Farrell moving to inside centre. Ford would assume an even more important role after his captain received a dead leg and was unable to follow up his perfect eight out of eight kicks against Australia. Ford was more than up to the kicking challenge and delivered another of what was a series of excellent performances at the World Cup.

The sustained England assault put the All Blacks on the back foot and it was no surprise when the 2003 champions crossed the try line after just two minutes with centre Manu Tuilagi picking the ball up and plunging over, leaving Farrell a simple conversion. Ford kicked a long-range penalty on 40 minutes but thanks to the Underhill try being ruled out, England went in at half time wondering if 10–0 was going to be enough to hold off the inevitable fight-back.

Crucially, England took the early initiative in the second half and although that line-out mistake allowed Savea to score with Richie Mo'unga's conversion reducing the lead to 13–7, Farrell made sure his players did not panic or go into their shells. Ford added two more penalties to give him 12 points. The impressive Nigel Owens continued to communicate effectively with the players and was forced to issue a final warning to birthday boy Kieran Read, the All Blacks' captain, about the number of offences his men were committing. It was that kind of day for the All Blacks.

While the defending champions lost their discipline, England showed a confidence under pressure that delighted Jones who recognised that his players had just outplayed an outstanding New Zealand outfit and he said: 'I thought Owen [Farrell] and the leaders on the field were absolutely exceptional. They kept the team discipline, kept our game plan, kept attacking where we thought New Zealand were weak and we didn't divert from that.'

At the heart of the England performance was that man Itoje, who made more than 10 tackles, won three vital turn-overs, and never took a backward step. It showcased why he is regarded as the outstanding player of his generation. In contrast, Brodie Retallick, for some years considered to be the best lock in world rugby, was eclipsed and appeared still to be short of game time after his serious shoulder injury, while his partner Sam Whitelock had a nightmare match, being penalised at one point for knocking over Farrell.

The England captain made the most of the incident, which didn't please some of the All Blacks, but it hardly mattered in a game where England came of age as a rugby force and the All Blacks were shown to be human after all.

Jordie Barrett tries to make inroads in England's defence with support from Sonny Bill Williams, but is held by Mark Wilson and Maro Itoje.

NEW ZEALAND 7		ENGLAND 19	
1 Joe Moody	13 Jack Goodhue	1 Mako Vunipola	13 Manu Tuilagi
2 Codie Taylor	14 Sevu Reece	2 Jamie George	14 Anthony Watson
3 Nepo Laulala	15 Beauden Barrett	3 Kyle Sinckler	15 Elliot Daly
4 Brodie Retallick		4 Maro Itoje	
5 Sam Whitelock	*Replacements*	5 Courtney Lawes	*Replacements*
6 Scott Barrett	16 Dane Coles	6 Tom Curry	16 Luke Cowan-Dickie
7 Ardie Savea	17 Ofa Tuungafasi	7 Sam Underhill	17 Joe Marler
8 Kieran Read (c)	18 Angus Ta'avao	8 Billy Vunipola	18 Dan Cole
	19 Patrick Tuipuloto		19 George Kruis
9 Aaron Smith	20 Sam Cane	9 Ben Youngs	20 Mark Wilson
10 Richie Mo'unga	21 T. J. Perenara	10 George Ford	21 Willi Heinz
11 George Bridge	22 Sonny Bill Williams	11 Jonny May	22 Henry Slade
12 Anton Lienert-Brown	23 Jordie Barrett	12 Owen Farrell (c)	23 Jonathan Joseph

Semi-Final 2
WALES DENIED AGAIN

by CHRIS JONES

Afterwards, there were plenty of Welsh tears, but no excuses. They knew they could have won, but in the end they were beaten by a stronger, marginally better side.

The parallels are so glaringly obvious that they border on the downright spooky. Four years ago at Twickenham, an injury-ravaged Wales lost a bitterly fought World Cup quarter-final by a single score when the Springboks made the decisive intervention with five minutes left on the clock. Spool forward to Yokohama in 2019 and what did we find? An injury-ravaged Wales losing another bitterly fought World Cup knock-out tie – this time a semi-final – by a single score when the same opponents struck at almost precisely the same moment in the contest. For all the talk of 'gods' from the England coach Eddie Jones over the course of the tournament, it was the men in red shirts who had most cause to ponder the motives of the sporting deities.

It was cruel. Not because Wales had in any way played the South Africans off the park before losing 19–16: to be blunt, they had barely played at all for long spells of the game, just as rugby of a positive nature had been close to non-existent for much of their last-eight victory over the French in Oita. No, it was cruel because the reigning Six Nations champions and Grand Slam winners were competing more through raw guts, pride and instinct than they were in the physical sense. Having been denied the services of three prime contenders for first-choice status before the tournament – the outside-half Gareth Anscombe, the flanker Ellis Jenkins and the number 8 Taulupe Faletau – and three more during it in the contrasting shapes of the full-back Liam Williams, the lock Cory Hill and the all-purpose loose forward

RIGHT South Africa winger S'Busiso Nkosi is held by flanker Justin Tipuric (L) and fly-half Dan Biggar.

BELOW RIGHT Damian de Allende finishes off his try despite the efforts of Welsh defenders.

BELOW Faf de Klerk looks to kick into space down the blind side of a scrum.

Josh Navidi, they took the field against the Boks with both centres, Jonathan Davies and Hadleigh Parkes, in conditions best described as orthopaedically challenged and then saw the celebrated wing George North and the senior tight-head prop Tomas Francis invalided out of the match before the interval. Had they somehow found their way into the final in the face of these odds, the selectors may have been forced to pick themselves.

Losing North to a hamstring injury was particularly damaging, for the two-time Lions tourist was fast rediscovering the best of himself after a spell in the doldrums – a dip in form so alarming for Warren Gatland, the head coach, that he was struggling to remain an automatic choice. After falling short as an 'influencer', to borrow the word said to be 'trending' amongst social media practitioners, during the pool stage, the big Ospreys game-breaker was certainly hungry for work and fully engaged now that a place in the final was in view. If the opening 40 minutes was very much a meat-and-one-veg affair offering multiple helpings of red-blooded arm-wrestling between the packs, together with a side portion of kicking from Gareth Davies and Faf de Klerk, the rival scrum-halves, the least claustrophobic moments involved the likes of North and his fellow wing Josh Adams, with the super-intelligent Jonathan Davies doing everything in his restricted power to facilitate them.

But these were isolated forays into the wide open spaces. The Boks were punishingly direct up front, with the stand-out number 8 Duane Vermeulen doing precisely what his opponents expect him to do without having much of an idea how to stop him, and the flanker Pieter-Steph du Toit bringing his mighty engine to bear on events more significantly than at any prior point in the competition. And then there was Damian de Allende, one of the most eye-catching of all World Cup centres for those who know what they are watching. Time and again, the midfielder from Western Province made metres on the carry, and in a game where every last centimetre of ground was fought over with blood-curdling intensity, his contribution was highly significant.

There was never more than a converted try between the sides. Handré Pollard, quite some marksman by any standards when his radar is in full working order, opened the scoring just shy of the quarter-hour when Wales, ultra-disciplined in their back-foot duties during the early exchanges, finally committed the cardinal rugby sin of compounding an error. A collision between Gareth Davies and Leigh Halfpenny as they attempted to deal with a box-kick from De Klerk handed the Boks an attacking scrum and at the ensuing ruck, Justin Tipuric was penalised after finding himself trapped on the floor by his rival flanker Siya Kolisi. Biggar's like-minded response from Willie le Roux's offside encroachment levelled things up, but then Pollard's double strike from either side of the field gave the South Africans just a hint of breathing space.

Pieter-Steph du Toit arrives too late to stop Josh Adams scoring his team's try as it seemed Wales might fight back.

The first of those penalty awards was questionable. Du Toit, jaw-dropping in his ground coverage but not always a paragon of discipline, clattered Ross Moriarty in the air a split-second after the Welshman had fumbled his attempted catch – a hit that might have resulted in a yellow card, but was not deemed worthy of a check by the French referee Jérôme Garcès and his fellow officials. The Boks were therefore left with an excellent scrum position and the heat they generated resulted in a mass disintegration of the Welsh set-piece and a shot at the sticks.

Ken Owens, quite brilliant at hooker in almost all respects, then conceded another penalty to the Boks at a maul and it was not until an off-the-ball hit on Aaron Wainwright, slightly less of a force on the flank than he had been in earlier matches but a revelation nonetheless, that Biggar was able to close the deficit to three points late in the half.

All to play for, then. Could Wales, roughed up in the forward exchanges but resilient and resourceful as the day is long, stay in touch until the last knockings and force the Springboks into a destructive bout of self-questioning? It looked like it when Biggar drew his men level with a penalty shortly after the restart, but then seemed much less likely when De Allende

RIGHT Lock Jake Ball and scrum-half Faf de Klerk in an exchange of pleasantries.

BELOW Rhys Patchell just fails in a drop-goal attempt, as De Klerk as usual makes things difficult for the opposition.

battered his way past both Welsh half-backs for the opening try on 56 minutes. Much of the approach work was down to the formidable Malcolm Marx, fresh on the field with his fellow front-rowers Steven Kitshoff and Vincent Koch, and Pollard, also involved in the build-up, maximised the score by nailing his conversion.

Biggar's fluffed tackle on De Allende would be his last act. On came Rhys Patchell, a very different kind of outside-half with very different ideas on how to shape an attacking game, and this was the signal for some long-awaited boldness with ball in hand. After laying siege to the Springbok line for what was almost forever, the Wales captain Alun Wyn Jones spurned a guaranteed three points in search of a gambler's seven. What was more, he rejected the usual line-out option by calling a scrum under the South African posts. A scrum? Against an off-the-bench Springbok unit with everything still in the tank? With a second-choice prop on the tight head in Dillon Lewis and the 21-year-old Rhys Carré, nothing more than a babe in swaddling clothes, on the loose head? If this was madness, there was method in it. Moriarty may have had to dig deep to drag the ball out of the set-piece, but the chaos wrong-footed the massed ranks of defenders and allowed Tomos Williams and Jonathan Davies to open up a path to the line for Adams with beautifully timed passes going left. Halfpenny's touchline conversion was a vintage effort and suddenly, Wales were back at 16-all and feeling chipper.

Unfortunately for them, the errors that almost always decide matches of this nature were theirs and theirs alone. Just as Wales were building for a late assault on the South African line, they lost control of a ruck and allowed Francois Louw, one of the great breakdown poachers of the age, to eke out a turn-over penalty and create a golden opportunity for the Boks to maul their opponents into the Japanese dirt. They set about this task with their customary ruthlessness; the Welsh forward retreat was too chaotic for the liking of referee Jérôme Garcès; and Pollard, cucumber-cool with the boot as he had been all night, kicked the winning points.

Afterwards, there were plenty of Welsh tears, but no excuses. They knew they could have won, but also knew they were not the victims of injustice. The last time they had played a World Cup semi-final, in Auckland in 2011, they lost by a point to the French after losing their captain, Sam Warburton, to an early red card – a decision that remains hotly debated to this day. This was different. They were beaten by a stronger, marginally better side. Does that hurt more, or less? Only they can say.

ABOVE LEFT R. G. Snyman secures a line-out, supported by fellow replacements Steven Kitshoff (R) and Francois Louw.

LEFT South Africa start to celebrate at the final whistle as Welsh heads finally drop.

RIGHT Duane Vermeulen (in Welsh shirt) and Willie le Roux enjoy the winning moment.

WALES 16		SOUTH AFRICA 19	
1 Wyn Jones	13 Jonathan Davies	1 Tendai Mtawarira	13 Lukhanyo Am
2 Ken Owens	14 George North	2 Mbongeni Mbonambi	14 S'Busiso Nkosi
3 Tomas Francis	15 Leigh Halfpenny	3 Frans Malherbe	15 Willie le Roux
4 Jake Ball		4 Eben Etzebeth	
5 Alun Wyn Jones (c)	*Replacements*	5 Lood de Jager	*Replacements*
6 Aaron Wainwright	16 Elliot Dee	6 Siya Kolisi (c)	16 Malcolm Marx
7 Justin Tipuric	17 Rhys Carré	7 Pieter-Steph du Toit	17 Steven Kitshoff
8 Ross Moriarty	18 Dillon Lewis	8 Duane Vermeulen	18 Vincent Koch
	19 Adam Beard		19 R. G. Snyman
9 Gareth Davies	20 Aaron Shingler	9 Faf de Klerk	20 Franco Mostert
10 Dan Biggar	21 Tomos Williams	10 Handré Pollard	21 Francois Louw
11 Josh Adams	22 Rhys Patchell	11 Makazole Mapimpi	22 Herschel Jantjies
12 Hadleigh Parkes	23 Owen Watkin	12 Damian de Allende	23 Frans Steyn

The Semi-Finals
WHAT THEY SAID

ENGLAND 19 NEW ZEALAND 7

England coach Eddie Jones   'New Zealand are the God of rugby, so we had to take it to them. To try to put them on the back foot as much as we could. They have got a great coach and great captain. They kept fighting to the end. We had to dig deep to win.

'Our tactical discipline was good and our defence work-rate was good. Most of the time we attacked well but missed a couple of opportunities.

'We've come here to be the world's best and we haven't done that yet.'

England captain Owen Farrell   (*On the haka*) 'We wanted to keep a respectful distance but we didn't want to just stand in a flat line.

'We went from the off. We've got a number of ways of playing; a big pack but they can play as well.'

England centre Manu Tuilagi   'We just keep focused and carry on, get your second wind and that way you get through it. Against the All Blacks it's never done until the final whistle. It doesn't matter how many points you are ahead you cannot take your foot off the gas. We gave it everything.'

England flanker Sam Underhill   'You have got to be good at something and I can't kick. Defence is always a good indicator of where a team is at mentally because the majority of it is just effort. This is the best experience of my life, never mind rugby. It is a bit surreal at the moment because we are in the final but I have loved every minute of it.'

England prop Mako Vunipola   (*About England standing up to the haka*) 'We wanted to be respectful, but also make sure they knew we were ready for the fight. We knew it would rile them up – it probably felt like we disrespected them. We meant no offence by it – we just wanted to let them know we were ready for the challenge ahead.'

England lock Maro Itoje   'It was definitely a top, top game. We played some good rugby for the most part and they really pushed us to be our best. I'm really happy with the win. We got the job done. If you want to win a game of rugby you have to win the breakdown and today was no different.'

England number 8 Billy Vunipola   (*About Sam Underhill and Tom Curry*) 'They just go all day. It allows me to rest so I can help in other ways. I just watch them. The work they put in is quite inspiring for me and the rest of the team. It is not just the hits but the turn-overs, the work with the ball, and for two lads that are quite young I hope they have many more caps.

'I don't know who started going to the gym earlier between the two of them but those boys started early. Unders doesn't have a neck as his back is so big, and Curry is the same. He's massive. They're smashing it.'

New Zealand coach Steve Hansen   'They had guys who were prepared to throw their bodies at our boys. They created the go-forward in the game. We struggled to dominate at breakdown time. When you are going forward you get all the 50–50 decisions. That is not an excuse, but it just happens. I think that the detail of the match didn't go our way but our work-rate and how much we really wanted it was there.

'Tonight is pretty gutting. When it doesn't go your way it is a hard thing to take. They are a good team and there is no shame in being beat but there is a lot of hurt.'

New Zealand captain Kieran Read   'I feel empty. It is a tough pill to swallow because of the effort you have put in and the guys beside me have put in.

Kieran Read, still bearing the evidence of a hard-fought contest, reflects on the result in a post-game interview.

New Zealand wing George Bridge 'They came out with a hiss and a roar, gave us a punch to the nose from the get-go.'

New Zealand scrum-half Aaron Smith 'You feel like you've let everyone down. I'm real gutted for New Zealand. But high-performance sport isn't fair and we fell on that end of the stick tonight.'

SOUTH AFRICA 19 WALES 16

South African coach Rassie Erasmus   'First of all I think it was a little bit of experience. When we analysed the way they won the Six Nations we saw they were a team that strangle the life out of the opposition. We received that and had to match that. It was nerve-racking at the end and I must say that, after losing the previous four matches against them, it could have gone their way again. It wasn't a great spectacle, but the boys stuck to their guns and adapted to that.'

South Africa captain Siya Kolisi   'I can't believe I'm here. I watched our last final in 2007 in a township tavern. You don't dream about that where I'm from. You are going to make mistakes. We weren't happy with our discipline in the first half. I thought we were putting them under pressure and then releasing it by giving away a penalty.'

South Africa fly-half Handré Pollard   'This is a very strong group. We've come a long way in the last two years. There have been a lot of new guys coming in. We've had 20 weeks of prep and now finally a World Cup final.'

Wales coach Warren Gatland   'South Africa deserved to win. They were very good up front, defended exceptionally. It was a real arm-wrestle. With 76 minutes on the clock and 16-all I thought we had a bit of momentum, but they got the turn-over and then the penalty. They had four penalties and that's the difference between winning and losing these tight games.'

Wales captain Alun Wyn Jones 'I am hurting. We are disappointed. The tighter games are usually attritional. Not until those last four or five minutes did we feel out of it. Today we fell short.'

Wales wing Josh Adams (leading try scorer in RWC) 'I would have given up all my tries to make the final.'

The expressions say it all: Warren Gatland and Alun Wyn Jones give post-match interviews.

The Bronze Final
A GAME TOO FAR FOR WALES

by **HUGH GODWIN**

There was so much for the illustrious pair to talk about as each of the two venerable coaches got ready to move on to the next chapter in his long career.

The time-honoured ritual of sharing a post-match beer was observed by Warren Gatland and Steve Hansen in Tokyo Stadium, after Hansen's New Zealand beat Gatland's Wales 40–17 to secure third place in the World Cup. And the immediate thought was whether one can of ale each would be nearly enough when there was so much for the illustrious pair to talk about – Hansen's team falling short of the 'three-peat' of World Cup titles, Gatland's men running out of steam as injuries found them wanting in their strength in depth, and each of the two venerable coaches moving on to the next chapter in his long career.

Hansen was pleased his team showed 'some real character and commitment to the jersey' on their reappearance after the shattering loss to England in the semi-final six days earlier, as he ended eight years as head coach, with a stint as assistant to Graham Henry before that. Hansen's future was believed to lie in the much less pressurised Japanese club league, as director of rugby at Toyota Verblitz, where he would be joined by the departing New Zealand captain and number 8, Kieran Read.

Ben Smith, a long-time maestro in the back three, was mostly overlooked by Hansen in this World Cup, but he showed his enduring class with surging finishes to two tries as the deposed champions built a 28–10 lead at half-time. The second of those scores was made by a pass beautifully threaded through the remnants of a line-out by Aaron Smith, the effervescent scrum-half. They were Ben Smith's 38th and 39th tries in Tests, which moved him beyond Jonah Lomu in sixth place on the all-time All Blacks list. Brodie Retallick's galloping break

in the fourth minute had sent Joe Moody on a rousing run-in, and full-back Beauden Barrett glided through from a switch pass by Aaron Smith, while Hallam Amos replied for Wales from Rhys Patchell's beautiful miss pass.

On a mild night, Sonny Bill Williams enjoyed himself with his off-loading, with Wales unable to muster the drive or muscle to stop this peerless aspect of the big centre's game. Ryan Crotty went over from one such intervention very early in the second half, before Wales celebrated their most significant moment of the match. A pleasing series of recycles, with the wing Josh Adams involved twice, ended with Adams dabbing the ball over the line round the side of a ruck for his seventh try of the World Cup, which put him two clear of Japan's Kotaro Matsushima and (after the final) one ahead of South Africa's Makazole Mapimpi at the top of the tournament's charts.

There followed a fallow period of 17 minutes before New Zealand's fly-half Richie Mo'unga threw a lavish sidestep to veer consummately round Dan Biggar, who had come on for Patchell in a reversal of Wales's first-choice routine, and complete the scoring.

Adams had agreed a transfer from Worcester to Cardiff Blues for the post-World Cup season, but the 24-year-old had previously drifted out of Wales and any contention for the national team until Gatland and his former backs coach Rob Howley identified him as a rough diamond worth polishing.

For Gatland himself, having seen his team edged out by South Africa in an attritional semi-final, a repeat of the fourth-place finish of 2011 was a decent return as he signed off 12 years in charge of Wales, ahead of his two new roles: a return to his native New Zealand to coach the Waikato-based Chiefs in Super Rugby, followed by a year with the British & Irish Lions up to and including the 2021 tour to South Africa.

Gatland was anticipating a formal farewell on Welsh soil when he coached the Barbarians against Wales in Cardiff at the end of November, but there was a poignant valedictory message here from the nuggety former Waikato hooker, who has also coached on three Lions tours since 2008. 'I have gone through that process of knowing it was my last game and not trying to get too emotional about it,' Gatland said. 'It is something I had prepared myself for, and then to start thinking about the next challenges in my life. We feel like we have put respect back into Wales as an international team and new coaches can come in and build on that. It would break my heart if Wales went back into the doldrums.'

His successor is another Kiwi, Wayne Pivac, whose backs coach Stephen Jones started work sooner than planned after replacing Rob Howley early in the piece in Japan.

Asked his advice for Pivac, Gatland replied: 'Putting family first. If things are right at home for the players, and we make the home life as easy we can, I know I get a better product on the training ground and on the rugby pitch. We haven't just talked about it, we've lived it … and it has given us a lot of returns.'

Wales's captain Alun Wyn Jones had been substituted during the second half, so for once did not look shattered during the after-match press interviews. 'His success has been unrivalled,' Jones said of Gatland, with whom he may yet work again in 2021. '[Three] Grand Slams and [two] semi-finals of the World Cup speak for themselves. That foundation is there, whereas it wasn't after the 2007 World Cup, plus an identity I mentioned in the changing room afterwards.'

Still there was the nut of New Zealand which Wales under Gatland never managed to crack. As Mo'unga finished with five conversions for a total of 15 points, Read the skipper completed an 11th win out of 11 in Tests against Wales – who have not beaten New Zealand since 1953.

Hansen departed with the best record of any coach who has been in charge for more than 15 Tests, having

won 92 matches, drawn 4 and lost 10, for an astonishing 88.64 per cent winning rate. His assistant Ian Foster said: 'He'll hit me if I get a bit gushy with him. He has been incredibly demanding on this group and the expectations have always been high, coupled with a massive amount of compassion and empathy with the individual. I can't say any higher than he has added to a legacy [of the All Blacks] that means a lot to him.'

Steve Hansen (L) and Warren Gatland meet up for that post-match beer and no doubt reflect on what might have been.

NEW ZEALAND 40		**WALES 17**	
1 Joe Moody	13 Ryan Crotty	1 Nicky Smith	13 Jonathan Davies
2 Dane Coles	14 Ben Smith	2 Ken Owens	14 Owen Lane
3 Nepo Laulala	15 Beauden Barrett	3 Dillon Lewis	15 Hallam Amos
4 Brodie Retallick		4 Adam Beard	
5 Scott Barrett	*Replacements*	5 Alun Wyn Jones (c)	*Replacements*
6 Shannon Frizell	16 Liam Coltman	6 Aaron Wainwright	16 Elliot Dee
7 Sam Cane	17 Atunaisa Moli	7 Justin Tipuric	17 Rhys Carré
8 Kieran Read (c)	18 Angus Ta'avao	8 Ross Moriarty	18 Wyn Jones
	19 Patrick Tuipuloto		19 Jake Ball
9 Aaron Smith	20 Matt Todd	9 Tomos Williams	20 Aaron Shingler
10 Richie Mo'unga	21 Brad Weber	10 Rhys Patchell	21 Gareth Davies
11 Rieko Ioane	22 Anton Lienert-Brown	11 Josh Adams	22 Dan Biggar
12 Sonny Bill Williams	23 Jordie Barrett	12 Owen Watkin	23 Hadleigh Parkes

The Final
SOUTH AFRICA TAKE THE TITLE

by **MICK CLEARY**

Apart from a couple of sequences, England never looked like getting across the tryline. South Africa did and they came good when it mattered.

England came with such hope, such conviction, such expectation. That sense of buoyancy lasted all of three minutes, the time it took for Kyle Sinckler to slump to the turf after his head struck the hip of Springbok wing Makazole Mapimpi. Sinckler was out cold and so, as it turned out, were England. From the heights of their semi-final win over the All Blacks to the depths of despair against the Springboks, England saved their worst for last. It was a dismal end to what had been a wonderful tournament for them.

They had come into the match as warm favourites following their stunning win over the defending champions. As a measure of their self-assurance Eddie Jones named an unchanged starting XV for only the second time in his tenure. The head coach would have pondered a switch back to the midfield line-up that did so well against the muscular Wallaby runners in the quarter-final, trading fly-half George Ford for Henry Slade with Owen Farrell donning the number 10 shirt. 'Horses for courses,' Jones deemed the change at the time and it had certainly proved productive against Australia, England denying the Wallabies any purchase

Siya Kolisi and Tendai Mtawarira were among the South Africa players who gave a particularly emotional rendering of their national anthem.

LEFT It starts to go wrong for England. Kyle Sinckler is down, eyes already shut, as Makazole Mapimpi contests Maro Itoje's tackle.

BELOW LEFT England made all too many errors as well. Elliot Daly loses the ball in contact as Cheslin Kolbe tackles.

ABOVE Even the talismanic Billy Vunipola could make little headway against the likes of Eben Etzebeth (R).

across the gain line and Ford doing what he does best in the later stages, pinning the opposition back into the corners and using his distribution skills to take advantage of any openings.

But this was to be same-again bullish England going in against South Africa, emboldened not just by their victory over the back-to-back defending champions but by the tone of their whole journey to this point. Jones stated that he had spent four years planning for this World Cup denouement, and knew from the moment the draw was made in Kyoto two and half years earlier that it was likely that England would have to achieve a triple-whammy over the southern hemisphere in successive weekends if the Webb Ellis Cup was to be brought home. Australia had been put to the sword, likewise New Zealand, and South Africa remained between Jones's team and the sort of glory that still attaches itself to the boys of 2003 – Martin Johnson, Jonny Wilkinson, Lawrence Dallaglio *et al.*

It was tempting to say 'only' South Africa stood in the way as if the Springboks were somehow to be considered a formality in terms of gaining victory. After all, they had lost on the opening weekend of the tournament to the same New Zealand outfit that England had so comprehensively dismantled. No side had ever won a World Cup that had dropped a game earlier in the tournament. It was not, either, as if the Boks had arrived in the final on a surge of fine form, swatting aside opponents in the manner that all-conquering South Africa teams of history have managed, big, muscular outfits that dominate from first whistle to last. It had taken this Springbok team a long time to subdue the wonderful resistance of Japan in their quarter-final and they had only just managed to get past Wales in the closing five minutes in the semi-final despite having the better of the kick-and-chase game. South Africa had looked one-dimensional in that match, only capable of playing a tight, pressure game and hoping for purchase on the scoreboard from the considerable boot of fly-half Handré Pollard.

Oh we of little faith! There were undercurrents at work that ought to have been heeded in the build-up, notably the Siya Kolisi factor and its resemblance to the forces that came into play in the 1995 final when the

ABOVE Kickers win matches. Handré Pollard knocks over 3 points while Owen Farrell sees one slip past the post.

LEFT Eben Etzebeth keeps a move going with a back-handed off-load to Damian de Allende.

BELOW LEFT Faf de Klerk and Lukhanyo Am congratulate Makazole Mapimpi on his try.

Mandela Moment resonated throughout the Rainbow Nation as the Boks toppled favourites New Zealand. The symmetry between that occasion and the final at the International Stadium in Yokohama was profound. Kolisi was the first black captain of South Africa, a township boy who had to scrabble to find his next meal when he was growing up, hostage to all the ills that attended such an upbringing; yet he had come through adversity to become a symbol of hope throughout the land. Factor in, too, that South African president Cyril Ramaphosa had flown in the day before the final, accompanied by seven cabinet ministers, and

ABOVE RIGHT R. G. Snyman wins a line-out. Snyman and the other Springbok replacements kept the pressure up throughout.

RIGHT Malcolm Marx (16) and his fellow front rowers win clean possession in a scrum.

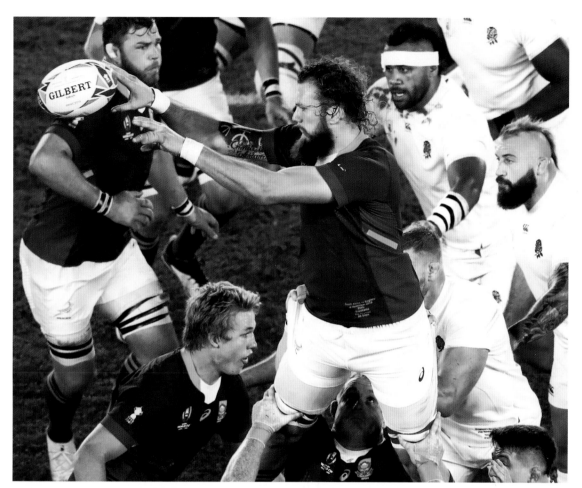

ABOVE Maro Itoje meets an immovable trio of Springbok tacklers.

TOP RIGHT Cheslin Kolbe steps inside Owen Farrell on the way to his try to finish off England's hopes.

RIGHT The final whistle and South African celebrations can begin in earnest.

presented the iconic number 6 Springbok shirt to Kolisi on the morning of the math.

So much for portents. There was still a match to play and contests to be won. Yet from the very first whistle there was an overwhelming sense of destiny as to what unfolded. This even extended to the bizarre fact that England were 20 minutes late in arriving at the stadium, only getting there with just less than an hour to spare. 'Traffic, don't you ever get caught up in traffic?' was the response from an RFU spokesman the following day as if a World Cup final were some sort of routine assignment.

England looked as rushed and frantic in those opening exchanges as if they had indeed just tumbled off the bus and on to the pitch. There was panic in their play, a failing that had simply not been there seven days earlier at the self-same stadium.

Self-assured one week, woe-begotten the next, unsure, uncertain, all at sea. Losing Sinckler to concussion after three minutes was a shock to England's system to compound their jittery state. The scrum was a disaster zone. Five penalties were conceded in that phase alone. Once again, putting back-to-back performances together from semi-final to final looked to be beyond a side.

South Africa had had the shorter turnaround from their semi-final win over Wales yet it was England who appeared lacking in energy. Rassie Erasmus identified minutes played of the respective front-rows throughout the tournament, the Springboks shuffling their resources astutely, as a possible factor. It certainly seemed that way, and it looked true all over the park.

Passes went astray. Line-outs were lost. Penalties were conceded. Scrums creaked and splintered. A restart was fluffed. George Ford kicked out on the full. Error upon error. It was as poor an opening as England have had in the entire tournament. Sinckler's absence was costly, although South Africa also lost two forwards in the first half: lock Lood de Jager and hooker Mbongeni Mbonambi.

England never did find any sort of composure, any sense of their old selves, much as they battled to stay in the fight. They were only 12–6 adrift at half-time which was some sort of accomplishment given how much under the cosh they had been. They were unable to get on the right side of referee Jérôme Garcès, who didn't like what he was seeing at the scrum and reacted accordingly. Dan Cole, no matter how reinvigorated across the year he had been, was not able to produce across a 77-minute shift. Joe Marler was sent into the fray early

in the second half to see if could shore up the scrum, lock George Kruis likewise. All to no avail. No team that has trailed at half-time in a World Cup final has ever managed to come back to win the game. England had a small window of opportunity midway through the second half when Sam Underhill managed to get purchase in the tackle and Owen Farrell knocked over his third penalty in the 51st minute to keep England within touching distance at 15–9, only to miss another reasonably straightforward pot at the posts three minutes later.

That was all South Africa needed, a little nudge in the ribs to remind them the final had not yet been won. Pollard struck his sixth penalty of the evening, before Farrell came back with another.

England, though, were hanging on but eventually the dam gave way as the Springboks delivered delirium to the country back home with two clinching tries in the closing 13 minutes.

Apart from a couple of sequences, England had never looked like getting across the tryline. South Africa did and they came good when it mattered, Mapimpi kicking and chasing and taking an inside pass from Lukhanyo Am to score. Seven minutes later, it was crackerjack wing Cheslin Kolbe who cut inside Owen Farrell to race away.

The captain was left on his backside, an image that somehow encapsulated England's night.

SOUTH AFRICA 32		ENGLAND 12	
1 Tendai Mtawarira	13 Lukhanyo Am	1 Mako Vunipola	13 Manu Tuilagi
2 Mbongeni Mbonambi	14 Cheslin Kolbe	2 Jamie George	14 Anthony Watson
3 Frans Malherbe	15 Willie le Roux	3 Kyle Sinckler	15 Elliot Daly
4 Eben Etzebeth		4 Maro Itoje	
5 Lood de Jager	*Replacements*	5 Courtney Lawes	*Replacements*
6 Siya Kolisi (c)	16 Malcolm Marx	6 Tom Curry	16 Luke Cowan-Dickie
7 Pieter-Steph du Toit	17 Steven Kitshoff	7 Sam Underhill	17 Joe Marler
8 Duane Vermeulen	18 Vincent Koch	8 Billy Vunipola	18 Dan Cole
	19 R. G. Snyman		19 George Kruis
9 Faf de Klerk	20 Franco Mostert	9 Ben Youngs	20 Mark Wilson
10 Handré Pollard	21 Francois Louw	10 George Ford	21 Ben Spencer
11 Makazole Mapimpi	22 Herschel Jantjies	11 Jonny May	22 Henry Slade
12 Damian de Allende	23 Frans Steyn	12 Owen Farrell (c)	23 Jonathan Joseph

The Final
WHAT THEY SAID

SOUTH AFRICA

Head coach Rassie Erasmus   (*On his team's scrum dominance*) 'I think it's a spin-off of the way we've played the previous five games. With our six forwards/two backs split on the bench, it's allowed us to keep our tight five fresh and especially with the six-day turn-around. Our six front-row forwards have had more or less the same amount of minutes and when you compare the time the England front row had, they've had heavy loads, playing 60 or 70 minutes in most games, with our boys playing 40 or 50 minutes. You spread that over five weeks of a World Cup and when you get to the semi-final and final, it takes its toll. I don't think their guys are bad scrummagers, I just think our guys were that bit fresher.'

Captain Siya Kolisi   'The coach told us before the last game that we were not playing for ourselves any more but for the people back home. We really appreciate all the support we've had from people in the townships, shebeens, on the farms and homeless. Thank you so much. We love you South Africa and we can achieve anything if we work together as one.'

Fly-half Handré Pollard   'We weren't perfect but it was good enough. We believe in the way we play and have played for two years. We know we are in with a chance if our forwards fetch up physically and today was unbelievable. This is really something special.'

Prop Tendai Mtawarira   (*About winning multiple scrum penalties*) 'That was too good to be true. Rugby is built around the set-piece and our scrum went well. It's something we have put a lot of focus on and we have made a lot of improvements. It was good to get a few penalties up front. The English have a great pack so they didn't make it easy, but we managed to get the ascendancy we wanted. Our set-piece is a vital part. It wins us penalties and it gives our whole team energy. I wanted to scrum the best I've ever scrummaged and give my team energy and inspire the guys around me.

'For my whole career I've been working towards this. I've had a few tough lessons, but every lesson I've had led to tonight.'

Winger Makazole Mapimpi   (*On scoring the first try*) 'I got the ball from Malcolm Marx. I saw that Lukhanyo Am was on my inside. I chipped the ball and he got the ball back. I saw that there as no one in front of me. I chased up and he gave me the ball to score.'

Scrum-half Faf de Klerk   'There are so many cool heads in our group and I think that was the difference. There was a lot of belief in our plan and what we can achieve. To see it all pan out in a final is amazing. We grew a lot after the loss to the All Blacks in the first game. That maturity shone through.

'We said from the start we wanted to play a game that can win finals. England tried to play from their own half and our defence was absolutely outstanding. When you see the forwards knocking the opposition back every time it really gives the backs confidence.'

ENGLAND

Head coach Eddie Jones   'We got in trouble at the scrum. We struggled, particularly in the first half.

'We made some personnel changes in the second half and got back into it, but again South Africa were too strong for us. We didn't think this was going to be the case, but that's what happens in rugby sometimes. You've got to be able to break the game open a bit and you have to be able to stay in the fight. I thought we stayed in the fight pretty well and at 50 minutes we were in with a chance but couldn't take our opportunities. They took their opportunities and that was the difference.

'I am not sure why we came up short today. Sometimes you can investigate but you will never know why it happened. We are going to be kicking stones now for four years.

'We did not meet our goal to be the best team in the world. But we are the second-best team in the world and I think that is how we should be remembered. The players prepared tremendously well. I thought they played with a lot of pride and passion and we got caught short. These things happen but we can't double the effort. I thought they were extraordinary.

'The silver medal is not as good as the gold medal but it's a silver medal. The players have conducted themselves brilliantly in Japan. They've been great ambassadors for English rugby.'

Captain Owen Farrell   'I am not sure what happened. It didn't feel that we had too much of a shot in the first half. It did get going in the second, but we probably took too long and then they managed to score a try. It's not just if set pieces go wrong, it's all aspects and they've all got to work to fall together and if one's not working another bit has to look after that but it didn't quite work like that.

'We are proud to have come as far as we have. Today didn't go our way but we've enjoyed this tournament."

Fly-half George Ford   We were massively inaccurate in the first half. When we had the ball we couldn't build any pressure. It's a hard one to take. You always want to get on the front foot but we can't fault our lads up front. They have been unbelievable all tournament. South Africa just got one up on us. It is tough when they get a lead like that and keep kicking the three.

'You have to chase the game in a match they are very good in. They executed their game plan brilliantly today.'

Scrum-half Ben Youngs   'It will take a long time to get over this defeat. We are devastated. It hasn't just been this tournament, it's been a huge lead-up.'

Prop Kyle Sinckler   (*Injured in the 3rd minute*) 'Words can't do justice to how I'm feeling. Biggest moment in my life and not even being able to get a chance to shoot my shot. Sport is cruel but we can never let adversity get the better of us. As a team we will come back stronger. Love playing with my brothers and I'll be back.'

Prop Mako Vunipola   (*Referring to Sinckler's injury*) 'It was just one of those things that happens quickly in rugby. You have got to move on quickly, but we didn't adjust to what they were doing quickly enough. At half-time we spoke about not waiting for them to put the ball in, maybe working a bit earlier. In that first scrum we didn't do that. We wanted to be the number 1 team in the world and we fell short, but we're still massively proud of what we achieved.'

Prop Joe Marler   'This team, if they keep developing as they have, they will dominate for a long period and that is a joy to see. They have got a bright future.'

Lock Maro Itoje   'We are trying to draw positives out of the journey. We are united, we are sticking together, we are talking and consoling each other. We want to get better and most of this squad will be at the next one. It is a long way away but our goal is to do better next time around.

'Losing this game was one of the most painful experiences that I have had in life, not just my rugby career. It is not easy.

'When a ram goes backwards it is not retreating, it moves back to gather more strength. A Nigerian proverb.'

Winger Jonny May   'There have been some great moments. I couldn't have done any more and the team couldn't have done any more.'

Your wealth.
Your family office.
Your way.

As a fifth-generation family office,
our first-hand experience brings real
understanding to your family's unique needs.

Investment Office | Real Estate | Corporate Finance | Private Equity | Family Office Services

RWC 2019: A Summary
'RUGBY SHOULD CREATE HOPE'

by CHRIS JONES

No other World Cup has seen half the host population tune in to watch their national team play. The challenge for rugby in Japan is to build on the enthusiasm and interest generated.

Outside the dressing rooms under the main Yokohama International Stadium stand an exchange took place after a pulsating final that summed up the special nature of Rugby World Cup 2019 in Japan. Siya Kolisi, the first black Springbok captain, who had only minutes earlier lifted the Webb Ellis Cup after a 32–12 triumph over England in the final, exchanged his number 6 jersey with 21-year-old Tom Curry, the England flanker, who came of age in the tournament.

The significance of the number 6 Springbok jersey in South African history is massive as President Nelson Mandela wore that number when he presented captain Francois Pienaar, in his own number 6, with the Cup in 1995. Now, 24 years later, the Rainbow Nation has another iconic image involving the famous jersey hopefully to use to help heal the differences and injustices still present in the country and which Springbok coach Rassie Erasmus highlighted when reflecting on an incredible achievement and a remarkable World Cup.

Erasmus, who admitted he was ready to quit as head coach a year ago due to the team's poor form, paid tribute to Kolisi, a boy who grew up in a township near Port Elizabeth, saying: 'In South Africa [pressure] is not having a job, having a close relative who is murdered. Rugby should not create pressure, it should create hope. We have a privilege, not a burden.

'It is easy to talk about going through hard times and struggling to get opportunities but it is tough when there are days when you didn't have food or couldn't go to school or didn't have shoes to wear. When you sit down and think about it, there was a stage when Siya didn't have food to eat and yes that is the captain and he led South Africa to hold this Cup and that is what Siya is.'

RIGHT A young fan remembers the late Chester Williams, the sole non-white Springbok in the 1995 winning team, who died shortly before RWC 2019 began.

BELOW Francois Pienaar and Siya Kolisi at the World Rugby Awards dinner, the day after the final. Unsurprisingly the Springboks were named as Team of the Year.

'Hope is when you play well and people watch the game and have a nice *braai* [barbecue] and watch the game and no matter of political or religious difference for those 80 minutes you agree when you usually disagree. That is our privilege and that was the way we tackled it.

'We decided we needed 20 weeks together to be competitive and it wasn't a sacrifice it was an honour and it's week 19 and the 20th week is the trophy tour in South Africa. A lot of people thought we couldn't make it but South Africans never give up and that makes us very proud.'

That South African pride delivered an awesome forward performance, supplemented by 22 points from outside-half Handré Pollard, who created a new individual scoring record for a Springbok at the World Cup. With six forwards and just two backs on the bench, the Springboks made no secret of what they intended to do to the England pack.

Without a platform and making too many errors in the face of the kind of defensive performance they had delivered while beating New Zealand 19–7 in the semi-finals, England could not get their game going. They were gracious in defeat, although in the immediate aftermath they could not explain how a normally solid scrum had fallen apart. It was a tough lesson for the youngest team in the professional era to compete in a Cup final, but one that will, hopefully, make them stronger in the coming years.

The Springboks headed home for their trophy tour having become the first team to win the Cup after losing a pool game – to New Zealand – and maintained their record of lifting the greatest prize in rugby every 12 years – 1995, 2007 and 2019.

Coach Erasmus is going 'upstairs' to oversee the next four years and the World Cup saw the end of other outstanding coaching regimes too, including Steve Hansen (New Zealand) Joe Schmidt (Ireland)and Warren Gatland (Wales). Their legacies are remarkable and the men who follow have huge boots to fill just as France face a major challenge to deliver a unique tournament in 2023. The French must try to match a spectacle that survived the ravages of Typhoon Hagibis, which forced the cancellation of three matches and caused widespread damage. Incredibly, the organisers got the Yokohama stadium ready just hours after nature's worst had halted the country so that Japan and Scotland could play their pool match. It was just one example of the 'can do' attitude that epitomised the tournament.

The World Cup was given a spectacular launch when Japan defeated Russia 30–10 in the opening Pool A match and reached an even greater fever pitch with their wonderful 19–12 win over an Ireland team that throughout the tournament looked like they had played their best rugby 12 months too soon. Ireland did account for a poor Scotland side 27–3 and would eventually finish runners-up as Japan held on for a breathless victory over Scotland 28–21 in Yokohama, where the locals had worked tirelessly to get the match on just hours after Typhoon Hagibis had forced the cancellation of the New Zealand v. Italy, England v. France and Canada v. Namibia matches. More than 80 deaths and 70,000 homes affected by flooding highlighted the danger the typhoon had posed.

Head coach Jamie Joseph and his Brave Blossoms fell at the quarter-final hurdle as South Africa gained revenge for their humiliating defeat in Brighton four years earlier. There would be no film made of this match but the bigger picture for Japanese rugby was more important. They had chances in the first half, thanks to their ability to play at a ferociously high tempo, but trailed 5–3 and that was never going to be enough as the Springboks used the second half to bring on even bigger forwards as they continued to pummel the opposition into submission.

Japan hit the wall – a green one – and could not sustain their level of performance for another 40 minutes and a 26–3 defeat was a fair reflection of how the game had gone. However, it took nothing away from what Joseph, his clever coaches and totally committed players had achieved during the tournament.

No other World Cup has seen half the population – 60 million – tune in to watch their national team play rugby but that happened in Japan and the challenge for everyone involved in the sport in the country is to build on the enthusiasm and interest generated. Gazing down from the 400 m Skytree tower in Tokyo you can clearly see the number of baseball diamonds in the city but you cannot see any rugby posts. Japan is baseball-mad and does not have a national schools programme or commitment to rugby and that is the real challenge for their rugby community – but at least they have been given a wonderful launch pad.

If Japan represented real improvement for a so-called Tier 2 nation, this World Cup was depressing for many of the countries who also labour under that banner.

In Pool B, Canada and Namibia spent the tournament with their eyes fixed on their meeting but it was cancelled leaving Phil Davies, the Namibia coach, unable to try and register the country's first ever World Cup victory in his final game. Canada would finish bottom of the pool on points difference with minus 163

Bundee Aki of Ireland tackles Ulupano Seuteni of Samoa: a red-card offence under the new policy regarding high tackles.

Veteran captains and leaders: Guilhem Guirado sees the funny side but Alun Wyn Jones is taking things more seriously.

while Namibia were minus 141. The pool was decided in the opening match with New Zealand battling back to defeat South Africa 23–13 and for Italy, the other team in the equation, it was a third-place finish and real disappointment that the cancelled game with New Zealand meant their outstanding captain Sergio Parisse had been denied his final Cup game before Test retirement.

The Typhoon's impact meant England finished top of Pool C without having to play France, who had somehow fought back to beat Argentina 23–21 in another example of Les Bleus' inconsistency. With England ending up playing against 14 men in the wins over USA and Argentina there was a feeling they had not been really tested before their resulting top place earned a knock-out match against Australia. France headed for their quarter-final with Wales while Argentina went home not having done themselves justice. The USA and Tonga fought it out for bragging rights, which the islanders claimed with a 31–19 win.

In Pool D, Fiji were expected to be a real threat to Wales and Australia, but came up short when it mattered most. They were badly undermined when a high shot from Reece Hodge put Peceli Yato out of the match with Australia. It was no comfort to Fiji when Hodge was later banned as Yato had been playing brilliantly and had to be helped off as the Wallabies rallied to win 39–21. Fiji then conspired to lose 27–30 to a spirited Uruguay team that was under-powered in the forwards but had goal-kicking expertise and a great team spirit with the win sending their players and the nation into raptures.

Unfortunately for Uruguay, while Fiji were found wanting, Georgia turned up with their full pack of forwards and smashed their way to a 33–7 win, although they would then feel the Fijian backlash when the Pacific Islanders delivered a Semi Radradra-inspired 45–10 victory that made their performance against Uruguay even harder to explain. Radradra scored two tries and helped make three others with one of the performances of the tournament. Fiji lost to Wales and the top two in the Pool was decided by Wales's 29–25 win over Australia. Wales led 23–8 with the help of a brilliant intercept try by Gareth Davies but it was Rhys Patchell, on for the injured Dan Biggar, whose kicks kept the Wallabies at bay in the later stages.

The quarter-finals saw Ireland limp out of the tournament against the All Blacks while Japan's challenge hit the buffers as South Africa outmuscled them in what would prove to be a portent of things to come in the final. England were too good for Australia while Sébastien Vahaamahina's sending off against Wales ruined his team's chances of making the final four. It was at the penultimate stage that England produced one of their greatest performances to outplay defending champions New Zealand 19–7 and Welsh coach Gatland suggested some teams leave their best in the semis and don't deliver in the final. He would be proved right.

Wales lost a kick fest semi-final with South Africa as that man Pollard guided his men into the last match of the tournament and left Gatland to face a bronze-medal clash with New Zealand that his injury-hit squad could not win. It gave Hansen and captain Kieran Read a winning send-off after truly outstanding careers.

Team of the Tournament
THE BEST OF RWC 2019

by SIR IAN McGEECHAN & IAN ROBERTSON

Siya Kolisi: 'To know this player, and his background, is to know, and admire his strengths. Quietly efficient and strong, … the oil to other cogs.'

1. Tendai Mtawarira Powerful scrummager and ball carrier who can dominate the close channels around ruck and maul. Creates important gain-line momentum.
Second choice: Mako Vunipola

2. Mbongeni Mbonambi Consistent line-out thrower who is powerful in the set-pieces. Good ball-carrier in phase play and very dangerous close to the line.
Second choice: Jamie George

3. Kyle Sinckler Ultra-dynamic and skilful forward. Creates momentum with his carries and clever running lines for others to benefit from, but also has great natural hands making him a threatening link player.
Second choice: Frans Malherbe

4. Maro Itoje His outstanding game awareness and involvement make him so important to the team dynamic, both in attack and defence. Very competitive and has now become the essential driver in England's forward play. Now as good as anybody in the world in his position.
Second choice: Eben Etzebeth

5. Alun Wyn Jones For effort, honesty, single-minded involvement and leading by example, there is no one better. His determination to get all the forward basics right, all of the time, makes him a tower of strength from whom others benefit.
Second choice: Lood de Jager

6. Siya Kolisi Captain. To know this player, and his background, is to know, and admire his strengths. Quietly efficient and strong, delivers accurately at key moments, making him the oil to other cogs. He performs with a consistency and accuracy, both in attack and defence, which removes any excuses for panic.
Second choice: Tom Curry

7. Pieter-Steph du Toit Powerful, clever and dynamic, Du Toit has been the leading edge in South Africa's all-consuming defensive speed, as well as the competitor at contact. Tremendous work rate and harries half-backs relentlessly. Selected as World Player of the Year 2019.
Second choice: Sam Underhill

8. Duane Vermeulen Powerhouse and go-to ball carrier. Tidies everything up in the back field and carries ball powerfully in the opposition half where he invariably wins the first contact and allows his half-backs to take tactical control of the next phase. Immense.
Second choice: Kieran Read

9. Faf de Klerk Bundle of competitive energy, the heartbeat and soul of his team. His huge game involvement and competitiveness means he affects all aspects of play, both in attack and defence.
Second choice: Aaron Smith

10. Handré Pollard Strong ball-carrying, combined with the ability to deliver accurate long passes and powerful kicks, makes him difficult to read, and stop. Provides great platforms for his forwards to work off. Goal-kicking accuracy makes him a match winner.
Second choice: **Owen Farrell**

11. Semi Radradra Incredibly agile, magical fast feet with a balance which only comes from the South Seas. Creates opportunities from nothing for himself and others.
Second choice: **Anthony Watson**

12. Damian de Allende Immensely strong ball-carrier with deceptively good feet and therefore always difficult to check. Can be a devastating try-scorer one on one with a defender inside the 22.
Second choice: **Owen Farrell**

13. Manu Tuilagi Powerful ball-carrier who has the ability to run very good, late angles at defenders. Consistently crosses the gain-line and brings support players, especially the back row, into play. Made very important tackles as well as support drives into wide rucks to allow others to carry on attacks.
Second choice: **Anton Lienert-Brown**

14. Kotaro Matsushima Very quick with outstanding acceleration giving him the ability and confidence to attack defensive lines. This invariably left the first defender behind whilst opening up space for himself and support players to run into. Exciting outcomes.
Second choice: **Cheslin Kolbe**

15. Beauden Barrett Most skilful and attacking back in world rugby. Sees opportunities early and is a threat whenever he gets the ball, whether it be counter-attack, blind-side plays or attacks down the wide channels. Beats the first defender with remarkable ease.
Second choice: **Liam Williams**

BEST PERFORMERS AT RWC 2019

Most Points Scored, Individual

1.	Handré Pollard	South Africa	69
2.	Owen Farrell	England	58
3.	Richie Mo'unga	New Zealand	54
4.	Yu Tamura	Japan	51
5.	Dan Biggar	Wales	41
6.	Josh Adams	Wales	35

Jonny Wilkinson (England) leads the all-time points table with 277. Handré Pollard is the highest-ranked of the players active in 2019, in 7th place with a total of 162.

Most Points Scored, Team

1.	South Africa	262
2.	New Zealand	250
3.	England	190
4.	Wales	189
5.	Australia	152
6.	Ireland	135

New Zealand top the all-time team points table with 2,552, over 750 ahead of Australia in second place.

Most Tries Scored, Individual

1.	Josh Adams	Wales	7
2.	Makazole Mapimpi	South Africa	6
3.	Kotaro Matsushima	Japan	5
4.	Ben Smith	New Zealand	4
5.	Julian Montoya	Argentina	4
6.	Kenki Fukuoka	Japan	4

Bryan Habana (South Africa) and Jonah Lomu (New Zealand) are joint top of the all-time tries table with 15. Keith Earls (Ireland) is the highest-ranked of the players active in 2019 with 8, tied for 18th place, though he did not score in 2019.

Most Tries Scored, Team

1.	New Zealand	36
2.	South Africa	33
3.	England	22
4.	Wales	22
5.	Australia	21
6.	Ireland	20

New Zealand top the all-time tries table with 347.

Tendai Mtawarira
1

Mbongeni Mbonambi
2

Kyle Sinckler
3

Maro Itoje
4

Alun Wyn Jones
5

Siya Kolisi
6

Duane Vermeulen
8

Pieter-Steph du Toit
7

Faf de Klerk
9

Handré Pollard
10

Damian de Allende
12

Manu Tuilagi
13

Kotaro Matsushima
14

Semi Radradra
11

Beauden Barrett
15

Jamie George
16

Mako Vunipola
17

Frans Malherbe
18

Eben Etzebeth
19

Sam Underhill
20

Aaron Smith
21

Owen Farrell
22

Liam Williams
23

Eastdil Secured

is proud to support

Wooden Spoon Rugby World

EASTDIL SECURED

THE REAL ESTATE INVESTMENT BANKING COMPANY

NEW YORK | LOS ANGELES | LONDON | SAN FRANCISCO | ATLANTA | BOSTON
CHICAGO | DALLAS | FRANKFURT | HONG KONG | SEATTLE | SILICON VALLEY
TOKYO | ORANGE COUNTY | WASHINGTON, D.C. | CHARLOTTE

The Fans' World Cup
WARMTH OF WELCOME

by DAVID STEWART

To witness the utter joy on display when the 'Brave Blossoms' scored thrilling tries against Scotland and when their quarter-final qualification was confirmed was a privilege.

There is so much to report. The editor was asked to make 10 pages available. He offered 1,000 words; I have just wasted 26 of them. Where to start: the tournament, or the country? In the modern colloquialism, visitors from the world's rugby nations – if this was their first experience of Japan – were 'blown away'. Particularly outside Tokyo, the cheeriness, helpfulness and warmth of welcome was a pleasure to behold. Family units found it an educational, culturally enriching experience; those travelling alone were enchanted in other ways – the duration and variety of after-dark entertainment took a few long-term tourists pleasantly by surprise!

Japan opened itself, probably as never before. We liked what we saw. One worldly Scotsman observed, ruefully, when standing on the spotlessly clean Shinkansen (bullet train) platform, 'They have maintained many of the standards and values we used to be known for, and increasingly seem to neglect.' He also had civil discourse in mind too: 'Respect seems something that is naturally given, rather than demanded – whether in street language or otherwise.' Lots of bowing and smiling – rapidly reciprocated.

A young Wales supporter, fully kitted out: Wales *v.* South Africa.

ABOVE The English take on the masked ninja : England *v.* All Blacks.

LEFT To scare the Springboks: Japan *v.* South Africa.

For some Japanese, this was a dry run for the Olympics. Not for their own rugby folk, though. To witness the utter joy on display when the 'Brave Blossoms' scored thrilling tries against Scotland – possibly the game of the tournament, in the widest sense – and at the final whistle, when their qualification as winners of Pool A was confirmed, was a privilege.

We shared their pleasure. South Africans working in the Middle East, Welshmen resident in North America, Irish in Australasia (where apparently they still learn the words to 'Fields of Athenry' – and sing it no matter who is playing), Scots from Hong Kong and Singapore, a Frenchman claiming heritage from the Borders ('I am a Gordon' … perhaps it was the gin). Class reunions, 50th anniversary trips, dads and lads sneaking away during half-term – the World Cup was a melting pot like never before, new friendships being kindled all around.

We tried to learn bits of the language, *arigato* (thank you) and *sayonara* (goodbye) being the most valuable, along with 'itchy, knee' (one, two). We learned about Shizuoka and Sapporo, and tried not to mix up Shinjuku, Shibuya, Shinagawa, and Shimbashi – all areas in downtown Tokyo. We became partial to *yakitori*, *ramen*, *miso* soup, and *gyoza* (meat dumplings, best with soy sauce) – at breakfast, and dinner; we sidestepped Starbucks and KFC. We got soaked to the skin one day, and relished late October shorts and T-shirt weather the next.

SNAPSHOTS

TOP LEFT Warm-up act: drummers parading round the stadium before kick-off.

TOP RIGHT Springbok fans, pre-match.

RIGHT Before Wales v. South Africa.

BOTTOM LEFT A Scotsman explains to Japanese TV what he keeps in his sporran.

BELOW Members of a Japanese rugby club who have temporarily switched loyalties to back Russia.

We drank in their pubs, which tend to be small; the shortage of real estate is well known. They have names like the Lord Nelson (Hamamatsu) and the Man on the Moon (Kyoto). They met with the approval of an 81-year-old brewing industry veteran who supports Exeter Chiefs, and a 14-year-old hooker from Wakefield. The sight and sound of this young thruster absorbing tales of yesteryear from front-rowers 40 years (Morpeth) and 60 years (Stirling) his senior was something to behold.

We loved listening to Matt Burke ('England will beat New Zealand') and Mike Tindall share their thoughts behind closed doors, along with the delightfully witty – perhaps understandably demob-happy – Wayne Barnes.

We checked our emotions when emerging from the relative darkness of a beautifully presented narrative on the August 1945 atom-bomb attack at the Peace Museum, into the light of a thriving 21st-century Hiroshima.

We sympathised with Jaco Peyper. Had he ignored those Welsh supporters in a hotel lobby, he stood accused of being rude or elitist. Instead, he did the friendly fun thing, posed for a quick photo; and the RWC authorities dumped on him. As with much else, Warren Gatland called it correctly: 'How people interpret that is up to them. Obviously, the way things are – how PC everyone is – people like to make mountains out of molehills.'

They got other things wrong as well. The typhoon which blew through east-central Japan on the last weekend of the pool stages led to the cancellation of three matches (from eight listed), notwithstanding the 'contingency plans' they told us were in place. Rescheduling? Namibia against Canada on the Sunday may not have meant much to television executives, but a heck of a lot to the players involved, their friends and families who had travelled a long way – whither that duty of care?

Supporters in organised tour groups felt short-changed at times. At smaller venues, favoured hotel locations went to tournament executives and administrators, teams and match officials, sponsors and media, while the travelling spectator – often the chairman/secretary/treasurer/coach of a local club – paying for packages including match tickets, put together by RWC, sometimes found him/herself out in the boondocks and behind the posts.

Gripes aside, how to summarise such a surprising, invigorating, compelling six weeks, when the fraternity of rugby came en masse to Asia for the first time?

Internationally, a favourite moment. Departing the Yokohama stadium after that vintage England semi-final performance, a chunky fellow of about 30 waved his arms by way of illustration while addressing me in his Hispanic-accented English: 'Rugby, what a wonderful game it is, I wish I could play.' Presuming him for perhaps an Argentinian or Uruguayan, my enquiry as to why not was met with 'I am from Guatemala …'

Domestically, interviewed in the *Japan Times*, a Mr Shiratori confessed he had only recently taken an interest in rugby, but he was not alone. 'Everyone's a fan now,' he said. 'It's such a great sport. The way the players hit each other hard but then show sportsmanship at the end. And the same goes for the visiting supporters – they have been so friendly. It's been an honour to watch rugby with them.'

Mr S., the feeling was mutual.

LEFT Homeward, tae think again; Japan v. Scotland.

BELOW Irish eyes are smiling: Samoa v. Ireland.

We are delighted to be supporting Wooden Spoon and would like to thank everyone for their dedication and devotion. If you would like to find out more about Artemis, please contact your financial adviser, call 0800 092 2051 or visit artemisfunds.com.

ARTEMIS
The PROFIT Hunter

RESULTS AND FIXTURES

3

A Summary of the Season 2018–19

by TERRY COOPER

INTERNATIONAL RUGBY

AUTUMN TOURS (2018)

NEW ZEALAND TO JAPAN & EUROPE

Japan	W 69–31
England	W 16–15
Ireland	L 9–16
Italy	W 66–3

Played 4 Won 3 Lost 1

AUSTRALIA TO WALES, ITALY AND ENGLAND

Wales	L 6–9
Italy	W 26–7
England	L 18–37

Played 3 Won 1 Lost 2

ARGENTINA TO IRELAND, FRANCE AND SCOTLAND

Ireland	L 17–28
France	L 13–28
Scotland	L 9–14

Played 3 Lost 3

OTHER AUTUMN INTERNATIONALS

Wales	21	Scotland	10
Ireland	54	Italy	7
Italy	28	Georgia	17
Scotland	54	Fiji	17
Wales	74	Tonga	24
England	35	Japan	15
Ireland	57	USA	14
France	14	Fiji	21

GUINNESS SIX NATIONS CHAMPIONSHIP 2019

Italy	16	Ireland	26
France	27	Scotland	10
Wales	21	England	13
England	44	France	8
Scotland	13	Ireland	22
Italy	15	Wales	26
Scotland	33	Italy	20
Ireland	20	England	32
France	19	Wales	24
Italy	14	France	25
Wales	25	Ireland	7
England	38	Scotland	38
Ireland	26	France	14
Scotland	11	Wales	18
England	57	Italy	14

	P	W	D	L	F	A	PD	B	Pts
Wales	5	5	0	0	114	65	49	0	23
England	5	3	1	1	184	101	83	4	18
Ireland	5	3	0	2	101	100	1	2	14
France	5	2	0	3	93	118	25	2	10
Scotland	5	1	1	3	105	125	20	3	9
Italy	5	0	0	5	79	167	88	0	0

UNDER-20 SIX NATIONS 2019

Ireland	35	England	27
Scotland	22	Italy	32
France	32	Wales	10
Scotland	5	Ireland	24
England	31	France	19
Italy	12	Wales	42
Italy	14	Ireland	34
Wales	11	England	10
France	42	Scotland	27
Ireland	31	France	29
Scotland	27	Wales	20
England	35	Italy	10
Italy	31	France	35
England	45	Scotland	7
Wales	17	Ireland	26

	P	W	D	L	F	A	PD	TB	LB	Pts
Ireland	5	5	0	0	150	92	58	3	0	26
France	5	3	0	2	157	130	27	4	1	17
England	5	3	0	2	148	82	66	3	1	16
Wales	5	2	0	3	100	107	-7	1	1	10
Italy	5	1	0	4	99	168	-69	2	1	7
Scotland	5	1	0	4	88	163	-75	2	0	6

WOMEN'S SIX NATIONS 2019

Ireland	7	England	51
Scotland	7	Italy	28
France	52	Wales	3
Scotland	5	Ireland	22
Italy	3	Wales	3
England	41	France	26
Italy	29	Ireland	27
France	41	Scotland	10
Wales	12	England	51
Scotland	15	Wales	17
England	55	Italy	0
Ireland	17	France	47

England	80	Scotland	0
Wales	24	Ireland	5
Italy	31	France	12

	P	W	D	L	F	A	PD	TB	LB	Pts
England	5	5	0	0	278	45	233	5	0	28
Italy	5	3	1	1	91	104	13	3	0	17
France	5	3	0	2	178	102	76	4	0	16
Wales	5	2	1	2	59	126	-67	1	0	11
Ireland	5	1	0	4	78	156	-78	2	1	7
Scotland	5	0	0	5	37	188	-151	0	1	1

RBS RUGBY EUROPE UNDER-18 CHAMPIONSHIP

(played in Russia)

Third place play-off

Portugal	38	Russia	27

Final

Georgia	23	Spain	10

WORLD RUGBY UNDER-20 CHAMPIONSHIP

(played in Argentina)

Third-place play-off

Italy	29	Georgia	17

Final

France	24	Australia	23

WORLD RUGBY PACIFIC NATIONS CUP 2019

Fiji	10	Samoa	3
USA	20	Japan	34
Tonga	33	Canada	23
Tonga	7	Japan	41
Fiji	38	Canada	13
USA	13	Samoa	10
USA	47	Canada	19
Japan	34	Fiji	21
Tonga	17	Samoa	25

Winners: Japan

WORLD RUGBY NATIONS CUP 2019

(Held in Montevideo, Uruguay in June)

Final

Uruguay	28	Argentina	15

THE RUGBY CHAMPIONSHIP 2018

Argentina	34	Australia	45
South Africa	30	New Zealand	32
Argentina	17	New Zealand	35
South Africa	23	Australia	12
Australia	19	Argentina	23
New Zealand	34	South Africa	36
Australia	23	South Africa	18
New Zealand	46	Argentina	24
Argentina	32	South Africa	19
New Zealand	40	Australia	12

South Africa	34	Argentina	21
Australia	13	New Zealand	38

	P	W	D	L	PD	BP	Pts
New Zealand	6	5	0	1	93	5	25
South Africa	6	3	0	3	6	3	15
Australia	6	2	0	4	-52	1	9
Argentina	6	2	0	5	-47	0	8

Champions: New Zealand

THE RUGBY CHAMPIONSHIP 2019

(A shortened competition due to World Cup – and also used as warm-up)

South Africa	35	Australia	17
Argentina	16	New Zealand	20
Australia	16	Argentina	10
New Zealand	16	South Africa	16
Australia	47	New Zealand	26

(Also Bledisloe Cup match 1)

Argentina	13	South Africa	46
New Zealand	36	Australia	0

(Also Bledisloe Cup match 2

South Africa	24	Argentina	18

	P	W	D	L	PD	B	Pts
South Africa	3	2	1	0	51	2	12
Australia	3	2	0	1	9	0	8
New Zealand	3	1	1	1	-17	0	6
Argentina	3	0	0	3	-43	2	2

Winners: South Africa
Bledisloe Cup Winners: New Zealand (points difference)

WORLD CUP WARM UP MATCHES (AUGUST AND SEPTEMBER 2019)

Ireland	29	Italy	10
England	33	Wales	19
France	32	Scotland	3
Italy	85	Russia	15
Wales	13	England	6
England	57	Ireland	15
Scotland	17	France	14
France	47	Italy	19
Georgia	10	Scotland	44
Wales	17	Ireland	22
England	37	Italy	0
Scotland	36	Georgia	9
Ireland	19	Wales	10

England: Played 4 Won 3 Lost 1

France: Played 3 Won 2 Lost 1

Ireland: Played 4 Won 3 Lost 1

Italy: Played 4 Won 1 Lost 3

Scotland: Played 4 Won 3 Lost 1

Wales: Played 4 Won 1 Lost 3

CLUB, COUNTY AND DIVISIONAL RUGBY

ENGLAND

Gallagher Premiership

	P	W	D	L	F	A	TB	LB	Pts
Exeter	22	17	0	5	630	438	14	4	86
Saracens	22	16	0	6	644	440	10	4	78
Gloucester	22	13	1	8	587	515	10	4	68
Northampton	22	11	0	11	590	521	8	4	56
Harlequins	22	10	0	12	544	528	7	9	56
Bath	22	10	2	10	481	480	6	6	56
Sale	22	11	2	9	462	504	3	4	55
Wasps	22	10	0	12	483	552	7	4	51
Bristol	22	9	1	12	503	580	6	7	51
Worcester	22	9	0	13	491	557	6	4	46
Leicester	22	7	0	15	478	632	5	8	41
Newcastle	22	6	0	16	395	541	1	6	31

Relegated: Newcastle

Play-offs
Semi-finals

Exeter	47	Northampton	12
Saracens	44	Gloucester	19

Final

Exeter	34	Saracens	37

Aviva A League

Northern Conference
Winners: Newcastle   Runners-up: Northampton
Southern Conference
Winners: Saracens   Runners-up: Exeter

Play-offs

		Semi-finals	
Saracens	89	Northampton	7
Newcastle	54	Exeter	12
		Final	
Saracens	55	Newcastle	14

Greene King IPA RFU Championship

	P	W	D	L	PD	B	Pts
London Irish	22	20	0	2	495	19	99
Ealing Trailfinders	22	17	0	5	230	18	86
Bedford Blues	22	13	0	9	29	17	69
Jersey	22	12	0	10	112	15	63
Cornish Pirates	22	10	0	12	49	19	59
Yorkshire Carnegie	22	11	0	11	-74	11	55
Nottingham	22	10	1	11	-89	10	52
Coventry	22	9	1	12	-140	13	51
London Scottish	22	8	0	14	-148	11	43
Doncaster	22	8	0	14	-71	10	42
Hartpury	22	7	0	15	-219	8	36
Richmond	22	6	0	16	-174	9	33

Promoted to Premiership: London Irish

National Leagues

National 1
Champions: Ampthill Runners-up: Old Elthamians

National 2 (S)
Champions :Rams   Runners-up: Canterbury

National 2 (N)
Champions: Hull Ionians   Runners-up: Chester

Play-off - National 2 N & S

Canterbury	19	Chester	10

Women's Premiership 15s
Play-off

Saracens	33	Harlequins	17

Women's Senior Cup Final

Leeds	20	Castleford	14

RFU Knockout Trophy Finals

Senior Vase

Honiton	29	North Allerton	27

Intermediate Cup

Kenilworth	32	Matson	26

Junior Vase

Leeds Weybridge	42	Thornesians	5

County Championship Finals

Division One (Bill Beaumont Cup)

Cornwall	14	Cheshire	12

Division Two

Leicestershire	38	Surrey	13

Jason Leonard National Under-20 Championship

Surrey	43	Berkshire	16

University Matches

Varsity Match

Oxford	38	Cambridge	8

Women's Varsity Match

Oxford	5	Cambridge	8

BUCS Competitions

Men's Champions:	Hartpury
Women's Champions:	Exeter 1st

Inter-services Championship

The Army	27	Royal Navy	11
The Army	49	Royal Air Force	3
Royal Navy	25	Royal Air Force	10

Babcock Trophy Winners: The Army

Hospitals Cup

Winners: Guy's

Schools

HSBC Rosslyn Park Schools Sevens

Open:	Sedbergh
U-14 Cup:	Harrow School
Plate:	Coleg Sir Gar
U-14 Plate:	Radley College
Girls' Schools :	Exeter College

Natwest Schools Cup Finals

Under-18 Cup Winners:	Whitgift School
Under-18 Vase Winners:	Whitgift School
Under-15 Cup Winners:	Wellington

SCOTLAND

Tennent's Premiership

	P	W	D	L	F	A	Pts
Ayr	18	14	0	4	516	287	71
Heriot's	18	13	1	4	569	293	67
Currie	18	13	0	5	536	368	67
Melrose	18	12	1	5	533	341	62
Watsonians	18	12	0	6	441	344	57
Stirling County	18	8	0	10	409	487	46
Boroughmuir	18	8	0	10	471	409	44
Glasgow Hawks	18	3	0	15	339	644	20
Hawick	18	4	0	14	251	586	19
Edinburgh Acads.	18	2	0	16	284	590	14

Tennents Premiership Play-off

Semi-finals

Heriot's	37	Currie	0
Ayr	15	Melrose	12

Final

Ayr	29	Heriot's	23

Tennent's National League Division 2

Winners: Biggar

Scottish National Cup:

Semi-finals

Hawick	19	Stirling County	51
Watsonians	10	Melrose	17

Final

Ayr	45	Heriot's	12

Shield Final

Aberdeen Grammar	26	Highland	10

Scottish Sevens Winners:

Kelso:	Watsonians
Selkirk:	Boroughmuir
Melrose:	London Scottish
Hawick:	Jed-Forest
Berwick:	Watsonians
Langholm:	Watsonians
Peebles:	Jed-Forest
Gala:	Edinburgh Academicals
Earlston:	Watsonian
Jed-Forest:	Watsonians

Kings of the Sevens: Watsonians

Women's Leagues

Premier League:	Hillhead Jordanhill
National League 1:	Ayr
National League 2:	Kelso

Sarah Beaney Cup

Winners: Watsonians

WALES

Welsh Principality Premiership

	P	W	D	L	F	A	TB	LB	Pts
Merthyr	30	23	0	7	885	591	23	2	117
Cardiff	30	22	1	7	991	660	17	4	111
Pontypridd	30	22	0	8	1015	580	18	4	110
Llandovery	30	21	1	8	854	551	15	3	104
Ebbw Vale	30	20	1	9	762	594	9	4	95
Aberavon	30	18	2	10	420	534	10	4	90
Newport	30	17	2	11	757	700	11	5	88
RGC 1404	30	14	1	15	859	650	16	11	85
Swansea	30	16	0	14	674	594	13	4	81
Carmarthen	30	13	1	16	637	584	8	9	71
Bridgend	30	12	0	18	689	714	9	9	66
Llanelli	30	12	1	17	679	723	10	3	63
Bedwas	30	12	1	17	681	835	8	4	62
Cross Keys	30	5	1	24	586	1093	9	5	36
Bargoed	30	6	0	24	576	1003	8	3	35
Neath	30	1	0	29	406	1274	2	3	3*

National Championship

	P	W	D	L	F	A	TB	LB	Pts
Pontypool	22	22	0	0	759	336	18	0	106
Ystrad R'da	22	16	0	6	533	454	11	1	76
Narberth	22	16	0	6	501	377	6	3	73
CMU	22	13	1	8	559	416	8	4	66
Tata Steel	22	9	0	13	573	570	11	5	52
Trebanos	22	10	0	12	437	446	4	7	51
Maesteg Q.	22	11	0	11	405	479	2	3	49
Beddau	22	8	0	14	426	516	3	8	43
Bedlinog	22	7	1	14	401	502	5	7	42
N'castle Em.	22	7	0	15	422	599	6	5	39
Newbridge	22	6	1	15	385	518	3	7	36
Rhydyfelin	22	5	1	16	340	528	4	5	31

* Neath deducted 6 points for failing to fulfil fixtures against Bedwas and RGC 1404.

WRU National Cup

Cardiff	25	Merthyr	19

Swalec Plate

Brecon	23	Bonymaen	21

Swalec Bowl

Abergavenny	27	Oakdale	23

Women's Premiership

Winners: Pontyclun

IRELAND

Ulster Bank League Division 1A

	P	W	D	L	F	A	TB	LB	Pts
Cork Con.	18	15	0	3	495	269	12	1	73
Clontarf	18	13	0	5	442	295	7	3	62
Lansdowne	18	12	0	6	534	400	10	2	60
Dublin Univ.	18	11	1	6	432	402	8	2	56
Garryowen	18	9	0	9	352	432	4	2	42
U.C.D.	18	5	3	10	376	455	7	3	36
Young Munster	18	5	1	12	341	397	6	7	35
Terenure Coll.	18	7	0	11	327	440	4	3	35
U.C.C.	18	5	1	12	379	447	5	6	33
Shannon	18	5	0	13	316	457	4	4	27

Ulster Bank League Division 1B

	P	W	D	L	F	A	TB	LB	Pts
Ballynahinch	18	12	1	5	399	323	5	2	57
Old Wesley	18	11	1	6	407	290	5	3	54
Naas	18	10	1	7	395	319	7	4	53
Malone	18	10	0	8	357	274	4	6	50
Banbridge	18	9	0	9	364	344	6	5	47
St Mary's Coll.	18	9	0	9	438	424	6	3	45
Old Belvedere	18	8	1	9	353	359	6	4	44
City of Armagh	18	8	2	8	325	347	4	2	42
Buccaneers	18	6	0	12	374	441	6	6	36
Ballymena	18	4	0	14	278	569	2	3	21

Ulster Bank League Division 2A

Winners: Highfield

Ulster Bank League Division 2B

Winners: MIJ Barnhall

Ulster Bank All Ireland Bateman Cup

City of Armagh	21	Garryowen	45

All Ireland Junior Cup Final

Ashborne	16	Enniscorthy	11

Fraser McMullen U-21 Cup

Dublin Univ.	41	U.C.C.	24

All Ireland Women's League Div. 1

U.L. Bohemia

Women's All Ireland Cup

Blackrock College	5	U.L. Bohemians	17

Women's Inter-Provincial Series

Munster and Leinster (shared)

Round Robin: Enniscorthy

SOUTH AFRICA

Currie Cup 2018

Final

Sharks	17	Western Province	12

NEW ZEALAND

Mitre Cup 2018

Premiership Final

Auckland	40	Canterbury	33

Championship Final

Waikato	36	Otago	13

Heartland Champions 2018

Meads Cup:	Thames Valley
Lochore Cup:	Horrowhenna-Kapiti

Ranfurly Shield 2018

Holders: Otago

Otago	23	Waikato	19

ITALY

National Championship of Excellence

Semi-finals

Calvisano	24	Emilia	20
Rovigo	18	Petrarca Padova	9

Final

Calvisano	33	Rovigo	10

FRANCE

Top 14 play-offs

Semi-finals

Clermont	33	Lyon	13
Toulouse	20	La Rochelle	6

Final

Toulouse	24	Clermont	18

INTERNATIONAL CLUB COMPETITIONS

Guinness PRO14 Play-offs

Quarter finals
(played between teams ranked 2nd and 3rd
in the two conferences).

Ulster	21	Connacht	13
Munster	15	Benetton	13

Semi-finals

Glasgow Warriors	50	Ulster	20
Leinster	24	Munster	9

Final

Leinster	18	Glasgow Warriors	15

European Rugby Champions Cup

Quarter-finals

Edinburgh	13	Munster	17
Saracens	56	Glasgow	27
Leinster	21	Ulster	18
Racing	21	Toulouse	22

Semi-finals

Saracens	32	Munster	16
Leinster	30	Toulouse	12

Final

Leinster	10	Saracens	20

Amlin European Challenge Cup

Quarter-finals

Sale Sharks	20	Connacht	10
Worcester	16	Harlequins	18
La Rochelle	39	Bristol	15
Clermont Auvergne	61	Cardiff	31

Semi-finals

La Rochelle	24	Sale Sharks	20
Clermont Auvergne	32	Harleqins	27

Final

Clermont Auvergne	36	Harlequins	27

Super Rugby Tournament

Quarter-finals

Jaguares	21	Chiefs	16
Crusaders	38	Highlanders	14
Hurricanes	35	Bulls	28
Brumbies	38	Sharks	13

Semi-finals

Jaguares	39	Brumbies	7
Crusaders	30	Hurricanes	26

Final

Crusaders	19	Jaguares	3

SEVENS

IRB Sevens Series Finals 2018-19

Dubai

New Zealand	21	United States	5

South Africa (Cape Town)

Fiji	29	USA	15

New Zealand (Hamilton)

Fiji	38	USA	0

Australia (Sydney)

New Zealand	21	USA	5

USA (Las Vegas)

USA	27	Samoa	0

Canada (Vancouver)

South Africa	21	France	12

Hong Kong

Fiji	22	France	7

Singapore

Fiji	28	Australia	22

England (Twickenham)

Fiji	43	Australia	7

France (Paris)

Fiji	35	New Zealand	24

Champions: Fiji

2018 World Rugby Women's Sevens

USA (Colorado)

New Zealand	33	USA	7

Dubai

New Zealand	26	New Zealand	14

Australia (Sydney)

New Zealand	34	Australia	10

Japan (Kitakyushu)

Canada	7	England	5

New Zealand (Langford)

New Zealand	21	Australia	17

France (Biarritz)

USA	25	New Zealand	10

Winners: New Zealand

BARBARIANS

Opponents	Results
Argentina (non cap)	W 38–35
England XV (non cap)	L 51–43

Played 2 Won 1 Lost 1

Fixtures 2019–20

NOVEMBER 2019

Sat 2	Rugby World Cup Final
Fri 1/Sat 2	Gallagher Premiership (3)
	RFU Championship Cup (4)
Fri 1–Sun 3	Guinness PRO14 (5)
	Greene King IPA Championship (4)
Sat 2	English National Leagues
	All Ireland Irish Leagues
	Welsh Principality Premiership
	Welsh National Leagues
Sun 3	Tennent's Scot. Women's P'ship
Fri 8–Sun 10	Gallagher English Premiership (4)
	Greene King IPA Championship (5)
	Scottish Super 6
Fri 8/Sat 9	All Ireland Irish Leagues
	Guinness PRO14 (6)
Sat 9.	English National Leagues
	Welsh Principality Premiership
	Welsh National Championship
	Welsh National Leagues
	Tennent's Scottish Premiership (8)
	Tennent's Scottish Leagues
Sun 10	Tennent's Scot. Women's P'ship
Fri 15–Sun 17	European Champions Cup (1)
	European Challenge Cup (1)
	Greene King IPA Championship (6)
Sat 16	BARBARIANS v FIJI
	ENGLAND v FRANCE (Women)
	English National Leagues
	Tennent's Scottish Premiership (9)
	Tennent's Scottish Leagues
	Scottish Super 6
	All Ireland Irish Leagues
	Welsh Principality Pemiership
	Welsh National Championship
	Welsh National Leagues
Fri 22–Sun 24	European Champions Cup (2)
	European Challenge Cup (2)
	Scottish Super 6
Sat 23	ENGLAND v ITALY (Women)
	English National Leagues
	Welsh Principality Premiership
	Welsh National Championship
	Welsh National Leagues
	Tennent's Scottish Premiership (10)
	Tennent's Scottish Leagues
Fri 29/Sat 30	All Ireland Irish Leagues
Sat 30	WALES v BARBARIANS
	English National Leagues
	Tennent's Scottish Premiership (11)
	Tennent's Scottish Leagues
	Welsh National Leagues

DECEMBER 2019

Fri 29 Nov–	Guinness PRO14 (7)
Sun 1 Dec	Gallagher English Premiership (5)
Sat 30 Nov.	Scottish Super 6
& Sun 1	Tyrrells Women's Premier 15s
Sun 1	Tennent's Women's P'ship S/Fs
Fri 6–Sun 8	European Champions Cup (3)
	European Challenge Cup (3)
	RFU Championship Cup (5)
Fri 6/Sat 7	HSBC World 7s Series (Dubai)
Sat 7/Sun 8	Scottish Super 6
	Tyrrells Women's Premier 15s
Sat 7	English National Leagues
	Tennent's Scottish Premiership (12)
	Tennent's Scottish Leagues
	Welsh Principality Premiership
	Welsh National Championship
	Welsh National Leagues
	All Ireland Irish Leagues
Thurs 11	Oxford Univ. v Cambridge Univ.
	(Men & Women)
Fri 13–Sun 15	European Champions Cup (4)
	European Challenge Cup (4)
	HSBC World 7s Series (Cape Town)
Fri 13/Sat 14	All Ireland Irish Leagues
	RFU Championship Cup (6)
Sat 14	English National Leagues
	Tennent's Scottish Premiership (13)
	Tennent's Scottish Leagues
	Welsh Principality Premiership
	Welsh National Championship
	Welsh National Leagues
Sat 14/Sun 15	Scottish Super 6
	Tyrrells Women's Premier 15s
Sun 15	Tennent's Women's P'ship F
Fri 20–Sun 22	Gallagher English Premiership (6)
	Greene King IPA Championship (7)
Fri 20/Sat 21	Guinness PRO14 (8)
Sat 21	Welsh Principality Premiership
	Welsh National Leagues
	Tennent's Scottish Leagues
Sat 21/Sun 22	Tyrrells Women's Premier 15s
Thu 26–Sat 28	Guinness PRO14 (9)
Fri 27–Sun 29	Gallagher English Premiership (7)
	(inc. The Big Game at Twickenham
	Harlequins v Leicester)
Sat 28	Welsh Principality Premiership
	Welsh National Championship
	Welsh National Leagues

JANUARY 2020

Fri 3–Sun 5	Gallagher English Premiership (8)
Fri 3–Sat 4	Guinness PRO14 (10)
Sat 4	English National Leagues
	Welsh Principality Premiership
	Welsh National Championship
	Welsh National Leagues
Fri 10–Sun 12	Greene King IPA Championship (8)
	European Champions Cup (5)
	European Challenge Cup (5)
Sat 11	English National Leagues
	Tennent's Scottish Premiership (14)
	Tennent's Scottish Leagues
	All Ireland Irish Leagues
	Welsh Principality Premiership
	Welsh National Championship
	Welsh National Leagues
Sat 11/Sun 12	
Tyrrells Women's Premier 15s	
Fri 17–Sun 19	Greene King IPA Championship (9)
	European Champions Cup (6)
	European Challenge Cup (6)
Sat 18/Sun 19	Scottish Super 6
	Welsh Principality Premiership
	Tyrrells Women's Premier 15s
Sat 18	English National Leagues
	Tennent's Scottish Premiership (15)
	Tennent's Scottish Leagues
	Welsh National Leagues
	Welsh National Championship
Fri 24–Sun 26	Greene King IPA Championship (10)
Sat 25	English National Leagues
	All Ireland Irish Leagues
Fri 24/Sat 25	Guinness PRO14 (8 – one match)
	Gallagher English Premiership (9)
Sat 25/Sun 26	HSBC World 7s Series (Hamilton)
	Scottish Super 6
Sat 25	Scottish Cup Q/F
	Welsh Principality Premiership
	Welsh National Championships
	Welsh National Leagues

FEBRUARY 2020

Fri 31 Jan/ Sat 1 Feb.	Gallagher English Premiership (10)
Fri 31 Jan– Sun 2 Feb.	Greene King IPA Championship (11)
Sat 1	WALES v ITALY (14.15)
	IRELAND v SCOTLAND (16.45)
	Premiership Rugby Cup SF
	English National Leagues
	Welsh National Leagues
	Guinness PRO14 (9 – one match)
Sat 1/Sun 2	HSBC World 7s Series (Sydney, Women)
Sun 1	FRANCE v ENGLAND (15.00)
Fri 7 /Sat 8	Premiership Rugby Cup SF
Fri 7–Sun 9	Greene King IPA Championship (12)
Sat 8	IRELAND v WALES (14:15)
	SCOTLAND v ENGLAND (16.45)
	English National Leagues
	Welsh National Leagues
	Premiership Rugby Cup SF

Sun 9	FRANCE v ITALY (15.00)
Fri 14–Sun 16	Greene King IPA Championship (13)
	Scottish Super 6
Fri 14/Sat 15	Guinness PRO14 (11)
	All Ireland Irish Leagues
	Gallagher English Premiership (11)
Sat 15	English National Leagues
	Premiership Rugby Cup F
	Welsh Principality Premiership
	Welsh National Championship
	Welsh National Leagues
	Tennent's Scottish Premiership (16)
	Tennent's Scottish Leagues
Fri 21/Sat 22	Gallagher English Premiership (12)
	All Ireland Irish Leagues
Fri 21–Sun 23	Guinness PRO14 (12)
Sat 22	ITALY v SCOTLAND (14.15)
	WALES v FRANCE (16:45)
	Welsh Principality Premiership
	Welsh National Leagues
Sun 23	ENGLAND v IRELAND (15.00)
Fri 28 Feb– Sun 1 Mar	Gallagher English Premiership (13)
	Greene King IPA Championship (14)
	Guinness PRO14 (13)
	Gallagher English Premiership (12)
Fri 28/Sat 29	All Ireland Irish Leagues
Sat 29	English National Leagues
	Tennent's Scottish Premiership (17)
	Tennent's Scottish Leagues
	Welsh Principality Premiership
	Welsh National Championship
Fri 28 Feb– Sun 1 Mar	HSBC World 7s Series (Los Angeles, Men)

MARCH 2020

Fri 6/Sat 7	Gallagher English Premiership (14)
Sat 7	IRELAND v ITALY (14.15)
	ENGLAND v WALES (16:45)
	English National Leagues
	Tennent's Scottish Premiership (18)
	Tennent's Scottish Leagues
	Welsh Principality Premiership
	Welsh National Leagues
Sat 7/Sun 8	HSBC World 7s Series (Vancouver, Men)
Sun 8	SCOTLAND v FRANCE (15:00)
Fri 13	Welsh Principality Premiership
Fri 13–Sun 15	Greene King IPA Championship (15)
Fri 13/Sat 14	All Ireland Irish Leagues
Sat 14	WALES v SCOTLAND (14.15)
	ITALY v ENGLAND (16.45)
	FRANCE v IRELAND (20.00)
	English P'ship Rugby Cup Final
Thu 19	Natwest Schools Cup Finals
Fri 20–Sun 22	Greene King IPA Championship (16)
	Scottish Super 6 Play-offs
Fri 20/Sat 21	Guinness PRO14 (14)
	Gallagher English Premiership (15)
	All Ireland Irish Leagues

Sat 21	English National Leagues
	Tennent's Scottish Premiership S/F
	Tennent's Scottish Leagues
	Welsh Principality Premiership
	Welsh National Championship
	Welsh National Leagues
Sat 21/Sun 22	Tyrrells Women's Premier 15s
Thu 26–Sat 28	All Ireland Irish Leagues
Fri 27/Sat 28	Gallagher English Premiership (16)
	(including Saracens v Harlequins at
	Tottenham Hotspur FC)
	Guinness PRO14 (15)
Fri 27 to	Greene King IPA Championship (17)
Sun 29	Scottish Super 6 Finals
Sat 28	English National Leagues
	Tennent's Scottish Leagues
	Scottish Cup SF
	Scottish National League Cup SF
	Scottish National Bowl SF
	Scottish National Shield SF
	Welsh Principality Premiership
	Welsh National Championship
	Welsh National Leagues
	Jason Leonard County U-20s QF
Sat 28/Sun 19	Tyrrells Women's Premier 15s

APRIL 2020

Wed 1.	Welsh National Leagues
Fri 3–Sun 5	HSBC World 7s Series
	(Hong Kong, Men)
	European Champions Cup Q/F
	European Challenge Cup Q/F
	Greene King IPA Championship (18)
Sat 4	English National Leagues
	Welsh Principality Premiership
	Welsh National Championships
	Tennent's Scottish Premiership F
Sat 4/Sun 5	Tyrrells Women's Premier 15s
Wed 8	Welsh National Leagues
Fri 10/Sat 11	Gallagher English Premiership (17)
	Guinness PRO14 (16)
Fri 10/Sun 12	Greene King IPA Championship (19)
Sat 11	Welsh National Championships
	Welsh National Leagues
Sat 11/Sun 12	Tyrrells Women's Premier 15s
	Jason Leonard County U-20s SF
Wed 15	Welsh National Leagues
Fri 17/Sat 18	Gallagher English Premiership (18)
	(inc. Bath v Wasps at Twickenham)
	Guinness PRO14 (17)
Sat 18	Welsh National Championships
	English National Leagues
	All Ireland Irish Leagues
	Welsh National Leagues
Sat 18/Sun 19	Tyrrells Women's Premier 15s

Wed 22	Welsh National Leagues
Fri 24–Sun 26	Gallagher English Premiership (19)
	Greene King IPA Championship (20)
Sat 25	Guinness PRO14 (18)
	English National Leagues
	All Ireland Irish Leagues
	Scottish Cup Final
	Welsh National Championships
Sat 25/Sun 26	Tyrrells Women's Premier 15s
Wed 29	Welsh National Leagues

MAY 2020

Fri 1–Sun 3	European Champions Cup S/F
	European Challenge Cup S/F
	Greene King IPA Championship (21)
Sat 2/Sun 3	HSBC World 7s Series
	(Langford BC, Women)
Sat 2	Welsh National Championships
	Welsh National Leagues
	Army v Navy (Babcock Trophy)
	Armed Forces U-23 v Oxbridge U
	U-23
Sun 3	RFU Junior Vase Final
	RFU Senior Vase Final
	RFU Intermediate Cup Final
	Jason Leonard County U-20s F
Fri 8–Sun 10	Greene King IPA Championship (22)
Fri 8/Sat 9	Guinness PRO 14 (19)
	All Ireland Irish Leagues
	English County Championship (1
	Welsh National Leagues
Fri 15/Sat 16	Guinness PRO 14 (20)
Sat 16	Gallagher English Premiership (20)
Sat 16/Sun 17	English County Championship (2)
Fri 22	Challenge Cup Final (Marseille)
Sat 23	Heineken Champions Cup Final
	(Marseille)
	English County Championship (3)
Sat 23/Sun 24	HSBC World 7s Series
	(London, Men)
Fri 29/Sat 30	Guinness PRO14 (21)
Sat 30/Sun 31	Gallagher English Premiership (21)
	HSBC 7S World 7s Series (Paris)

JUNE 2020

Sat 6	Gallagher English Premiership (22)
Sat 13	Gallagher English Premiership SF
Sat 20	Gallagher English Premiership F
	Guinness PRO14 F
Sun 21	English County Championship
	(Bill Beaumont Cup) Final
	Gill Burns Division 1 Final
	Bill Beaumont Div. 2 Final